New York Notary Public Exam

Explore Essential Knowledge for Exam Mastery
and Jumpstart Your New Career
[III EDITION]

Copyright © 2025 by Donald Bond

COPYRIGHT & DISCLAIMER

TABLE OF CONTENTS

1 GETTING STARTED WITH NOTARIZATION

1.1 Introduction to Notarization

Welcome to the fascinating and essential world of notarization. Whether you're embarking on a new career as a notary public or seeking to deepen your understanding of this vital profession, it's important to grasp the fundamental principles and responsibilities that come with the role. This chapter provides an introduction to notarization, offering a solid foundation upon which your notarial journey will build.

Understanding Notarization

Notarization is a formal process that serves to deter fraud and ensure the proper execution of important documents. A notary public, an impartial witness, verifies the identity of signers, ensures that they understand the contents of the document, and confirms that they are signing voluntarily. By doing so, notaries help maintain the integrity and legitimacy of countless transactions and legal processes.

The role of a notary public can be traced back to ancient Rome, where scribes, known as "notarii," recorded public proceedings and important transactions. These early notaries played a crucial role in the administration of justice and the preservation of legal records. Over time, the practice of notarization spread throughout Europe and eventually to the United States, where it became a respected and indispensable public office.

The Modern Role of Notaries

Today, notaries public are commissioned officials who perform a variety of important tasks. These include:

- **Acknowledgments**: Verifying that the person signing a document is indeed who they claim to be.
- **Jurats**: Administering oaths and affirmations to affirm the truthfulness of statements in documents.
- **Oaths and Affirmations**: Swearing in individuals for legal proceedings or official statements.
- **Certifying Copies**: Attesting that a copy of a document is a true and accurate reproduction of the original.
- **Affidavits**: Witnessing and certifying written statements made under oath.

- **Noting Protests**: Formally noting the dishonor of negotiable instruments such as checks or promissory notes.

These functions may seem straightforward, but they carry significant legal weight. A notary's certification provides assurance that a document is genuine, that its execution was not coerced, and that the parties involved are who they purport to be. This level of trust is crucial in various sectors, including real estate, finance, and law.

1.2 The Importance of Notaries in New York

In New York, notaries public play a vital role in maintaining the state's legal and business infrastructure. They are called upon to notarize documents that affect every aspect of life, from real estate transactions and business agreements to personal legal matters such as wills and powers of attorney. By ensuring the authenticity and integrity of these documents, notaries help prevent fraud and protect the interests of all parties involved. The demand for notarial services in New York is substantial. Every day, thousands of documents require notarization, underscoring the indispensable role that notaries play in the state's economy and legal system. This demand reflects the public's trust in notaries to uphold the highest standards of accuracy, impartiality, and professionalism.

1.3 Historical Context and Current Relevance

The office of the notary public has a rich history that underscores its enduring importance. As mentioned earlier, the origins of notarization date back to ancient Rome, where notaries were integral to the administration of justice. This tradition continued through the Middle Ages and into the modern era, with notaries becoming key figures in the documentation and authentication of important transactions.

In contemporary times, the role of the notary has expanded and adapted to meet the needs of a dynamic and increasingly digital world. The advent of remote notarization, for example, allows notaries to perform their duties via electronic means, making notarization more accessible and convenient without compromising security and authenticity.

Remote notarization involves using audio-visual technology to verify signers' identities and witness signatures in real-time. This innovation has proven especially valuable during the COVID-19 pandemic, enabling notaries to continue their work while adhering to social distancing guidelines. It also represents a significant step forward in the integration of technology into the notarial process, offering greater flexibility and efficiency.

Common Scenarios Requiring Notarization

To appreciate the practical importance of notarization, consider some common scenarios where notaries are needed:

- **Real Estate Transactions**: Notaries verify and witness the signing of deeds, mortgages, and other real estate documents, ensuring their validity and legality.
- **Legal Proceedings**: Affidavits, depositions, and other legal documents often require notarization to be admissible in court.
- **Financial Agreements**: Loan documents, contracts, and other financial instruments frequently need notarization to prevent fraud and confirm the parties' identities and intentions.

Personal Legal Matters: Wills, powers of attorney, and other personal documents require notarization to ensure they are executed properly and can be enforced. By providing these critical services, notaries public help uphold the rule of law and ensure the smooth functioning of society. Their work may often go unnoticed, but it is integral to the legal and commercial transactions that underpin our daily lives.

In conclusion, notarization is far more than a mere formality. It is a process steeped in history and vital to the integrity of modern legal and business practices. As a notary public, you will be entrusted with significant responsibilities, and your role will be essential in safeguarding the authenticity and reliability of important documents. Welcome to the world of notarization, your journey begins here.

2   THE PATH

2.1 Eligibility and Requirements

Embarking on the journey to become a notary public in New York State involves meeting specific eligibility criteria and requirements. Understanding these prerequisites is essential to ensure that you are qualified and prepared for the responsibilities that come with this important public office.

Basic Eligibility Criteria

To be eligible to become a notary public in New York, an applicant must meet the following basic criteria:

- **Age**: You must be at least 18 years old.
- **Residency**: You must be a resident of New York State or have an office or place of business in the state. Non-residents with a place of business within New York are also eligible.
- **Citizenship**: While you do not need to be a U.S. citizen, you must be a legal resident with the right to work in the United States.
- **Language Proficiency**: Proficiency in English is required, as all notarial acts and communications will be conducted in English.

Character and Background

In addition to the basic eligibility criteria, applicants must also meet certain character and background requirements:

- **Good Moral Character**: Applicants must demonstrate good moral character. This typically involves a background check to ensure there are no disqualifying criminal convictions.
- **Criminal History**: While a criminal record does not automatically disqualify an applicant, certain convictions, especially those involving fraud or dishonesty, may prevent you from becoming a notary. Each application is reviewed on a case-by-case basis.

Educational Requirements

New York State does not mandate formal education or specific training to become a notary public. However, possessing a good understanding of the duties and responsibilities of a notary public is crucial. Many applicants choose to complete a notary public course or study relevant materials to prepare for the notary public examination.

Professional Conduct and Competence

As a prospective notary public, you are expected to adhere to high standards of professional conduct and demonstrate competence in your duties:

- **Ethical Standards**: Notaries must perform their duties impartially and without bias. Any form of discrimination or conflict of interest must be avoided.
- **Understanding of Duties**: Applicants should be well-versed in the types of notarial acts they will be performing and the legal requirements for each. This includes understanding how to properly identify signers, administer oaths, and maintain accurate records.

Special Considerations

For certain professionals, additional considerations may apply:

- **Attorneys**: In New York, attorneys are automatically eligible to become notaries without the need to take the notary public examination. They must, however, submit the appropriate application and fee.
- **Court Clerks**: Court clerks of the Unified Court System, who have been appointed to their positions after taking a Civil Service promotional exam, are also exempt from the examination requirement.

Documentation and Fees

Applicants must submit specific documentation and fees as part of the application process:

- **Identification**: A valid photo ID, such as a driver's license or passport, is required to verify your identity.
- **Application Form**: The completed notary public application form must be submitted to the Department of State.
- **Fee**: The application fee, which is non-refundable, must accompany your application. As of this writing, the fee is $60, but applicants should verify the current fee before applying.

Step-by-Step Guide to Eligibility

1. **Verify Basic Criteria**: Ensure you meet the age, residency, and language proficiency requirements.
2. **Check Character and Background**: Be prepared for a background check and ensure you have a record of good moral character.

3. **Consider Education**: While not required, completing a notary course can be beneficial.
4. **Gather Documentation**: Collect the necessary identification and prepare to complete the application form.
5. **Understand Professional Standards**: Familiarize yourself with the ethical and professional standards expected of a notary public.
6. **Submit Application and Fee**: Complete the application process by submitting the form and fee to the Department of State.

Frequently Asked Questions (FAQs)

Q: Do I need to be a U.S. citizen to become a notary in New York? A: No, U.S. citizenship is not required. However, you must be a legal resident with the right to work in the United States.

Q: Can I become a notary if I have a criminal record? A: It depends on the nature of the conviction. While not all criminal records disqualify an applicant, convictions involving fraud or dishonesty are more likely to result in disqualification. Each application is reviewed individually.

Q: Is there a training course required to become a notary in New York? A: No formal training course is required by the state. However, many applicants choose to take a notary public course to better understand their duties and prepare for the examination.

Q: How long does the application process take? A: The processing time can vary. It is advisable to check with the New York Department of State for the most current information on application processing times.

Q: What happens if my application is denied? A: If your application is denied, you will receive a notification outlining the reasons for the denial. You may have the opportunity to address any issues and reapply.

By understanding and meeting these eligibility and requirement criteria, you can confidently proceed with your application to become a notary public in New York State. This foundational knowledge will ensure that you are well-prepared to undertake the responsibilities and duties that come with this important role.

2.2 Steps to Obtain a Commission

Once you have determined that you meet the eligibility and requirements for becoming a notary public in New York, the next step is to navigate the process of obtaining your notary commission. This involves a series of well-defined steps, from submitting your application to taking the notary public examination, and finally, receiving your commission. Below is a detailed guide to each step in the process.

Step 1: Prepare Your Application

The first step in obtaining your notary commission is to prepare your application. This involves gathering all necessary documentation and filling out the required forms.

- **Gather Required Documentation**:
  - Proof of identity (e.g., a valid driver's license or passport)
  - Proof of residency or place of business in New York State (e.g., utility bills, lease agreements)
  - For non-citizens, documentation of legal residency status
- **Complete the Application Form**:
  - Obtain the Notary Public Application form from the New York Department of State's website or office.
  - Fill out the form carefully, ensuring all information is accurate and complete. This includes your personal details, contact information, and any prior notary experience if applicable.
- **Application Fee**:
  - Include the non-refundable application fee with your completed form. As of this writing, the fee is $60, but it's advisable to check the latest fee schedule on the Department of State's website.

Step 2: Submit Your Application

Once your application form is complete and you have gathered all necessary documentation, you need to submit your application to the New York Department of State.

- **Submit by Mail or Online**:
    - You can submit your application by mail to the address provided on the form or, if available, through the online portal on the Department of State's website.
    - Ensure that you keep copies of your completed application and any receipts for your records.

Step 3: Prepare for the Notary Public Examination

After submitting your application, the next step is to prepare for the notary public examination. The exam tests your knowledge of the laws, procedures, and ethical responsibilities of a notary public.

- **Study Materials**:
    - Obtain the New York Notary Public License Law booklet, which contains the laws and regulations governing notaries in New York.
    - Consider enrolling in a notary public preparation course, which can provide comprehensive coverage of exam topics and practice questions.
- **Practice Tests**:
    - Take practice exams to familiarize yourself with the format and types of questions that will be on the actual test.
    - Review the answers and explanations to understand the reasoning behind each correct response.

Step 4: Take the Notary Public Examination

The notary public examination is a multiple-choice test that assesses your understanding of New York notary laws and procedures.

- **Scheduling the Exam**:
    - Check the exam schedule on the Department of State's website and choose a convenient date and location.
    - Register for the exam if required, following the instructions provided.
- **Day of the Exam**:
    - Bring a valid photo ID and any other required documentation to the exam site.

     o   Arrive early to ensure you have ample time to check in and get settled before the exam begins.
- **Taking the Exam**:
  - Read each question carefully and answer to the best of your ability. The exam typically covers topics such as notarial duties, ethical responsibilities, and legal requirements.
  - Manage your time efficiently to ensure you can complete all questions within the allotted time.

Step 5: Await Examination Results

After taking the exam, you will need to wait for your results. The New York Department of State will notify you of your exam results by mail.

- **Results Notification**:
  - If you pass the exam, you will receive a notice indicating your successful completion and further instructions for obtaining your commission.
  - If you do not pass, the notice will provide information on how to retake the exam.

Step 6: Receive Your Commission

Upon passing the notary public examination, you will receive your notary commission, which officially authorizes you to perform notarial acts in New York State.
- **Oath of Office**:
  - You will be required to take an oath of office, affirming your commitment to uphold the duties and responsibilities of a notary public.
  - This oath can typically be administered by a county clerk or another authorized official.
- **Receive Your Commission Certificate**:
  - After taking the oath, you will receive your official notary commission certificate. This document certifies your authority to act as a notary public.
- **Notary Seal and Supplies**:
  - Purchase a notary seal and other necessary supplies, such as a notary journal and stamps, from an authorized vendor. Ensure that your seal meets New York State requirements.

Step 7: Register with the County Clerk

Finally, you must register your notary commission with the county clerk's office in the county where you reside or have your principal place of business.

- **Submit Registration**:
    - Visit the county clerk's office with your commission certificate and any required fees.
    - Complete the registration process as directed by the clerk's office.
- **Receive Your Official Notary ID Card**:
    - Upon registration, you will receive your official notary public identification card. Keep this card with you when performing notarial acts.

Frequently Asked Questions (FAQs)

Q: How long is the notary public commission valid in New York? A: The notary public commission in New York is valid for four years. After this period, you must apply for renewal to continue performing notarial acts.

Q: Can I notarize documents before receiving my official commission? A: No, you must wait until you have received your official notary commission certificate and completed the registration with the county clerk before performing any notarial acts.

Q: Is the notary public examination difficult? A: The difficulty of the examination varies for each individual. Adequate preparation, including studying the Notary Public License Law booklet and taking practice tests, can significantly improve your chances of passing the exam.

Q: Can I transfer my notary commission to another state if I move? A: No, notary commissions are state-specific. If you move to another state, you will need to apply for a notary commission in that state according to its specific requirements.

Q: What happens if I lose my notary commission certificate or ID card? A: If you lose your notary commission certificate or ID card, you should contact the New York Department of State or your county clerk's office to obtain a replacement. There may be a fee associated with replacing these documents.

By following these detailed steps, you can navigate the process of obtaining your notary commission in New York with confidence. This structured approach ensures that you meet all legal requirements and are well-prepared to embark on your duties as a notary public.

2.3 The Application Process Explained

The application process to become a notary public in New York is a critical step that ensures all applicants meet the necessary qualifications and are prepared to fulfill their duties responsibly. This section provides a detailed explanation of the application process, from completing the form to submitting your application and preparing for the examination.

Step 1: Obtain the Application Form

The first step in the application process is to obtain the official Notary Public Application form from the New York Department of State. This form is available on the Department of State's website or can be requested from their office.

- **Accessing the Form**: Visit the New York Department of State's website and navigate to the notary public section to download the application form. Alternatively, you can contact the Department of State to have a form mailed to you.

Step 2: Complete the Application Form

Filling out the application form accurately and thoroughly is crucial. Ensure that all the information you provide is correct and up-to-date.

- **Personal Information**: Provide your full legal name, address, contact information, and date of birth. Ensure that the name you use matches the identification documents you will submit.
- **Residency Information**: Indicate your residency status and provide proof of residency or place of business in New York State.

- **Employment Information**: If applicable, include details about your current employment, especially if it relates to your duties as a notary public.
- **Character References**: Some forms may require character references or endorsements from reputable individuals who can attest to your good moral character.

Step 3: Prepare Supporting Documentation

In addition to the application form, you will need to gather and submit several supporting documents.

- **Proof of Identity**: Submit a copy of a valid photo ID, such as a driver's license, passport, or state-issued identification card.
- **Proof of Residency or Place of Business**: Provide documents such as utility bills, lease agreements, or business licenses that verify your residency or place of business in New York State.
- **For Non-Citizens**: Include documentation of your legal residency status in the United States, such as a green card or work visa.

Step 4: Submit the Application and Fee

Once your application form is completed and you have gathered all necessary documentation, you must submit your application to the New York Department of State along with the application fee.

- **Application Fee**: The application fee is currently $60, but it's advisable to check the latest fee schedule on the Department of State's website. This fee is non-refundable.
- **Submission Options**: You can submit your application by mail or, if available, through the online portal on the Department of State's website. If submitting by mail, ensure that you send your application to the correct address as specified on the form.
- **Keep Copies**: Make copies of your completed application form and all supporting documents for your records before submission.

Step 5: Await Confirmation and Examination Instructions

After submitting your application, you will receive confirmation from the New York Department of State. This confirmation will include instructions for scheduling and taking the notary public examination.

- **Confirmation Receipt**: Keep the confirmation receipt safe as it will contain important information regarding your examination.
- **Examination Scheduling**: Follow the instructions provided to schedule your examination. This may involve selecting a test date and location that is convenient for you.

Step 6: Prepare for the Notary Public Examination

Preparation for the examination is a crucial part of the application process. Ensure you have all the study materials and resources needed to pass the exam.

- **Study Materials**: Obtain the New York Notary Public License Law booklet, which contains the laws and regulations you need to know. Consider taking a preparation course if you feel you need additional guidance.
- **Practice Exams**: Take practice exams to familiarize yourself with the format and types of questions that will be on the actual test. Review the answers and explanations to ensure you understand the material thoroughly.

Step 7: Take the Notary Public Examination

The examination is a multiple-choice test that assesses your understanding of New York notary laws and procedures. It is essential to be well-prepared and to follow all instructions provided on the day of the exam.

- **Exam Day Requirements**: Bring a valid photo ID and any other required documentation to the exam site. Arrive early to ensure you have ample time to check in and get settled before the exam begins.
- **Exam Format**: The exam typically covers topics such as notarial duties, ethical responsibilities, and legal requirements. Manage your time efficiently to ensure you can complete all questions within the allotted time.

Step 8: Receive Examination Results

After taking the exam, you will need to wait for your results. The New York Department of State will notify you of your exam results by mail.

- **Passing the Exam**: If you pass the exam, you will receive a notice indicating your successful completion and further instructions for obtaining your commission.
- **Retaking the Exam**: If you do not pass, the notice will provide information on how to retake the exam. You can schedule another test date and continue your preparation.

Step 9: Receive Your Notary Commission

Upon passing the notary public examination, you will receive your notary commission, officially authorizing you to perform notarial acts in New York State.

- **Oath of Office**: You will be required to take an oath of office, affirming your commitment to uphold the duties and responsibilities of a notary public. This oath can typically be administered by a county clerk or another authorized official.
- **Commission Certificate**: After taking the oath, you will receive your official notary commission certificate. This document certifies your authority to act as a notary public.

Step 10: Register with the County Clerk

Finally, you must register your notary commission with the county clerk's office in the county where you reside or have your principal place of business.

- **Registration Process**: Visit the county clerk's office with your commission certificate and any required fees. Complete the registration process as directed by the clerk's office.
- **Notary Identification Card**: Upon registration, you will receive your official notary public identification card. Keep this card with you when performing notarial acts.

Frequently Asked Questions (FAQs)

Q: How long does the application process take? A: The processing time can vary, but it typically takes several weeks from the submission of your application to the receipt of your examination results. It is advisable to check with the New York Department of State for the most current information on processing times.

Q: Can I check the status of my application? A: Yes, you can contact the New York Department of State to inquire about the status of your application. They may provide updates or additional instructions if needed.

Q: What should I do if I need to update my application information? A: If you need to update any information on your application (e.g., address change), contact the New York Department of State promptly to ensure your records are accurate.

Q: Is there a fee for retaking the notary public examination? A: Yes, there is a fee for retaking the examination. The amount may vary, so check the current fee schedule on the Department of State's website.

Q: What should I do if I lose my commission certificate? A: If you lose your commission certificate, contact the New York Department of State to request a replacement. There may be a fee associated with issuing a new certificate.

By understanding and following this detailed application process, you can ensure that you meet all the necessary requirements and are well-prepared to become a commissioned notary public in New York State. This comprehensive guide provides the information and resources needed to navigate each step successfully.

2.4 Special Cases: Attorneys and Court Clerks

While the standard application process for becoming a notary public in New York involves meeting eligibility requirements, submitting an application, and passing the notary public examination, certain professionals may have unique pathways due to their existing qualifications. This section focuses on the special cases of attorneys and court clerks, detailing the streamlined processes available to them.

Attorneys

In New York State, attorneys are granted special consideration in the process of becoming notaries public. Recognizing their legal expertise and familiarity with legal documents and procedures, the state allows attorneys to bypass some of the standard requirements.

Eligibility for Attorneys:

- **Licensed Attorney**: You must be a licensed attorney in good standing with the New York State Bar.
- **Application Form**: Attorneys must complete the Notary Public Application form, but they are exempt from taking the notary public examination.
- **Proof of Status**: Include proof of your status as a licensed attorney, such as a copy of your attorney registration card or a certificate of good standing from the New York State Bar.

Steps for Attorneys:

1. **Complete the Application**: Fill out the Notary Public Application form with accurate and up-to-date information.
2. **Attach Proof of Status**: Include documentation that verifies your status as a licensed attorney in New York.
3. **Submit the Application and Fee**: Submit your completed application form, proof of status, and the application fee to the New York Department of State.
4. **Receive Your Commission**: Upon approval of your application, you will receive your notary public commission without the need to take the examination.
5. **Register with the County Clerk**: Complete the registration process with the county clerk's office in the county where you reside or have your principal place of business.

Court Clerks

Certain court clerks in New York are also eligible for a streamlined process when applying to become notaries public. This consideration applies to court clerks of the Unified Court System who have been appointed to their positions through a Civil Service promotional exam.

Eligibility for Court Clerks:

- **Appointed Court Clerk**: You must be an appointed court clerk in the Unified Court System of New York.
- **Civil Service Exam**: You must have been appointed to your position as a result of passing a Civil Service promotional exam.

Steps for Court Clerks:

1. **Complete the Application**: Fill out the Notary Public Application form with accurate and up-to-date information.
2. **Attach Proof of Status**: Include documentation that verifies your status as an appointed court clerk, such as a letter from your employer or a copy of your Civil Service exam results.
3. **Submit the Application and Fee**: Submit your completed application form, proof of status, and the application fee to the New York Department of State.
4. **Receive Your Commission**: Upon approval of your application, you will receive your notary public commission without the need to take the examination.
5. **Register with the County Clerk**: Complete the registration process with the county clerk's office in the county where you reside or have your principal place of business.

Additional Considerations for Attorneys and Court Clerks

While the streamlined process for attorneys and court clerks simplifies their path to becoming notaries public, it is important to note the following:

- **Oath of Office**: Like all notaries, attorneys and court clerks must take the oath of office, affirming their commitment to uphold the duties and responsibilities of a notary public.
- **Ethical Standards**: Attorneys and court clerks are held to the same high ethical standards and professional conduct as other notaries. They must perform their duties impartially and without bias.
- **Continuing Education**: While not mandatory, continuing education and staying informed about changes in notary laws and best practices are recommended for all notaries, including attorneys and court clerks.

Frequently Asked Questions (FAQs)

Q: Do attorneys need to take the notary public examination? A: No, licensed attorneys in good standing with the New York State Bar are exempt from taking the notary public examination.

Q: What documentation do court clerks need to provide with their application? A: Court clerks need to provide documentation that verifies their status as appointed court clerks in the Unified Court System, such as a letter from their employer or a copy of their Civil Service exam results.

Q: Are there any additional fees for attorneys and court clerks? A: Attorneys and court clerks are required to pay the standard application fee. There are no additional fees specific to their streamlined application process.

Q: Can attorneys and court clerks notarize documents immediately after receiving their commission? A: Attorneys and court clerks, like all notaries, must first complete the registration process with the county clerk's office before they can begin notarizing documents.

Q: Do attorneys and court clerks need to renew their notary commission? A: Yes, the notary commission is valid for four years, after which it must be renewed. The renewal process is the same for all notaries, regardless of their initial application process.

By understanding these special pathways, attorneys and court clerks can efficiently navigate the process of becoming notaries public in New York. This streamlined approach acknowledges their professional qualifications and ensures they are well-prepared to uphold the responsibilities of a notary public.

3   UNDERSTANDING THE EXAM

3.1 Exam Structure and Format

The New York Notary Public Exam is a critical step in obtaining your notary public commission. Understanding the structure and format of the exam is essential to ensure you are well-prepared and confident on test day. This section will provide a detailed overview of what to expect during the exam.

Exam Overview

The New York Notary Public Exam is a multiple-choice test designed to assess your knowledge of notary laws, procedures, and ethical standards as outlined in the New York Notary Public License Law. The exam is administered by the New York Department of State, Division of Licensing Services.

Key Details:
- **Exam Type**: Multiple-choice
- **Number of Questions**: 40 questions
- **Time Limit**: 1 hour
- **Passing Score**: 70% (28 correct answers out of 40)
- **Exam Fee**: Check the current fee on the New York Department of State's website

Exam Sections

The exam is divided into several sections, each covering different aspects of notarial practice. Understanding these sections will help you focus your study efforts on the most relevant areas.

1. **Notary Laws and Regulations**:
   - This section tests your knowledge of New York State laws governing notaries public, including the Notary Public License Law and related statutes.
   - Topics include eligibility requirements, notarial acts, prohibited conduct, and legal limitations.
2. **Duties and Responsibilities**:
   - This section assesses your understanding of the duties and responsibilities of a notary public.

- o Topics include administering oaths and affirmations, taking acknowledgments, executing jurats, and certifying copies.
3. **Ethical Standards**:
    - o This section evaluates your knowledge of the ethical standards and professional conduct expected of a notary public.
    - o Topics include impartiality, conflict of interest, confidentiality, and proper record-keeping practices.
4. **Procedures and Practices**:
    - o This section covers the practical aspects of performing notarial acts.
    - o Topics include verifying identities, maintaining a notary journal, handling remote notarizations, and using a notary seal.

Sample Questions

To help you prepare, here are a few sample questions that reflect the types of questions you might encounter on the exam:

1. **Notary Laws and Regulations**:
    - o **Question**: What is the term of a notary public commission in New York State?
        - A) 2 years
        - B) 4 years
        - C) 6 years
        - D) 10 years
    - o **Answer**: B) 4 years
2. **Duties and Responsibilities**:
    - o **Question**: Which of the following acts can a notary public perform?
        - A) Issue marriage licenses
        - B) Administer oaths and affirmations
        - C) Act as a real estate agent
        - D) Practice law
    - o **Answer**: B) Administer oaths and affirmations
3. **Ethical Standards**:
    - o **Question**: A notary public must maintain impartiality. Which of the following situations represents a conflict of interest?

- A) Notarizing a document for a friend
- B) Charging the maximum allowable fee for a notarization
- C) Notarizing a document in which the notary has a financial interest
- D) Keeping a detailed notary journal
  - **Answer**: C) Notarizing a document in which the notary has a financial interest
4. **Procedures and Practices**:
   - **Question**: What is the primary purpose of a notary journal?
     - A) To keep track of fees collected
     - B) To record the details of each notarial act performed
     - C) To provide a personal record for the notary
     - D) To advertise notary services
   - **Answer**: B) To record the details of each notarial act performed

Exam Registration and Logistics

- **Registration**: You can register for the exam through the New York Department of State's website. Ensure you complete the registration process and pay any applicable fees before the deadline.
- **Location and Schedule**: The exam is offered at various locations across New York State. Check the Department of State's website for the most current schedule and choose a location that is convenient for you.
- **Identification**: On the day of the exam, bring a valid photo ID, such as a driver's license or passport, to verify your identity.

Day of the Exam

- **Arrival**: Arrive at the exam location at least 30 minutes before the scheduled start time to allow for check-in procedures.
- **Materials**: You are not allowed to bring any study materials or electronic devices into the exam room. Scratch paper and pencils will be provided if needed.

- **Instructions**: Listen carefully to the instructions provided by the exam proctor. Make sure you understand the rules and format before beginning the test.

Scoring and Results

- **Scoring**: The exam is scored based on the number of correct answers. There is no penalty for guessing, so it is in your best interest to answer every question.
- **Results**: You will receive your exam results by mail. If you pass, you will be provided with instructions on how to complete the commissioning process. If you do not pass, you will receive information on how to retake the exam.

By understanding the structure and format of the New York Notary Public Exam, you can better prepare yourself for success. Focus your study efforts on the key sections and practice answering sample questions to build your confidence. The next sections will delve into the specific topics covered in the exam and offer strategies to help you prepare effectively

3.2 Key Topics Covered in the Exam

The New York Notary Public Exam covers a range of topics that are essential for performing the duties of a notary public effectively and legally. Understanding these key topics will help you focus your study efforts and ensure you are well-prepared for the exam. This section provides an overview of the primary subjects you need to master.

1. Notary Laws and Regulations

This section tests your knowledge of the legal framework governing notaries public in New York. It includes understanding the statutes, rules, and regulations that define and limit the powers of a notary.

- **Notary Public License Law**: Familiarize yourself with the New York Notary Public License Law, which outlines the responsibilities, limitations, and ethical standards for notaries.

- **Public Officers Law**: Understand the sections of the Public Officers Law that pertain to notaries, including the requirements for appointment and commission.
- **Real Property Law**: Know the provisions related to notarial acts in real estate transactions, such as acknowledgments and the recording of documents.
- **Executive Law**: Be aware of the Executive Law sections that address notarial acts, especially those related to authentication of documents.

2. Duties and Responsibilities

This section assesses your understanding of the core duties and responsibilities that a notary public must perform.

- **Administering Oaths and Affirmations**: Learn the procedures for administering oaths and affirmations, and understand the differences between them.
- **Taking Acknowledgments**: Understand the process of taking acknowledgments, including verifying the identity of the signer and ensuring they understand and willingly sign the document.
- **Executing Jurats**: Be familiar with jurats, which involve administering an oath or affirmation and witnessing the signing of a document.
- **Certifying Copies**: Know how to certify copies of documents, ensuring that the copy is a true and accurate reproduction of the original.

3. Ethical Standards

This section evaluates your knowledge of the ethical standards and professional conduct expected of a notary public.

- **Impartiality**: Understand the importance of acting impartially and avoiding conflicts of interest. Notaries must not perform notarial acts for close relatives or in situations where they have a personal or financial interest.
- **Confidentiality**: Maintain the confidentiality of the information and documents you handle. Notaries must not disclose details of a notarial act to unauthorized individuals.

- **Proper Conduct**: Adhere to the highest standards of professional conduct, including accuracy, diligence, and integrity in performing notarial acts.

4. Procedures and Practices

This section covers the practical aspects of performing notarial acts and the administrative requirements associated with them.

- **Verifying Identities**: Learn the methods for verifying the identities of signers, including the types of identification documents that are acceptable.
- **Maintaining a Notary Journal**: Understand the importance of keeping a notary journal and the information that must be recorded for each notarial act.
- **Using a Notary Seal**: Know the requirements for using a notary seal, including the information that must be included and the proper placement on documents.
- **Handling Remote Notarizations**: Be familiar with the procedures for performing remote notarizations, including the use of audio-visual technology to verify identities and witness signatures in real-time.

Sample Questions

To help you prepare, here are a few sample questions that reflect the types of questions you might encounter on the exam:

1. **Notary Laws and Regulations**:
   - **Question**: Under which law are notaries public in New York appointed?
     - A) Public Officers Law
     - B) Executive Law
     - C) Real Property Law
     - D) Judiciary Law
   - **Answer**: B) Executive Law
2. **Duties and Responsibilities**:
   - **Question**: What is the primary purpose of a jurat?
     - A) To certify that a document is a true copy of the original

- B) To certify that a signature was made in the presence of the notary
      - C) To affirm the truthfulness of the contents of a document under oath
      - D) To acknowledge that the signer understands and willingly signs the document
    - **Answer**: C) To affirm the truthfulness of the contents of a document under oath
3. **Ethical Standards**:
    - **Question**: Which of the following scenarios represents a conflict of interest for a notary public?
      - A) Notarizing a document for a colleague
      - B) Notarizing a document for a business partner
      - C) Charging the maximum allowable fee for a notarization
      - D) Keeping a detailed notary journal
    - **Answer**: B) Notarizing a document for a business partner
4. **Procedures and Practices**:
    - **Question**: What must be included in a notary journal entry?
      - A) The date and time of the notarial act
      - B) The fee charged for the notarial act
      - C) The type of notarial act performed
      - D) All of the above
    - **Answer**: D) All of the above

3.3 Preparation Tips and Strategies

Successfully passing the New York Notary Public Exam requires a combination of thorough preparation, effective study techniques, and practical strategies. This section provides essential tips and strategies to help you study effectively and approach the exam with confidence, utilizing the comprehensive resources provided in this book.

1. Create a Study Plan

A well-structured study plan is crucial for staying organized and ensuring you cover all necessary material.

- **Set Clear Goals**: Define what you need to achieve in each study session. Break down the material into manageable sections and set specific goals for each day or week.
- **Allocate Time Wisely**: Dedicate consistent, uninterrupted time for studying. Determine the best times of day for you to study and stick to your schedule.
- **Balance Topics**: Ensure your study plan covers all key topics, including notary laws, duties and responsibilities, ethical standards, and practical procedures.

3. Active Study Techniques

Engage actively with the material to enhance retention and understanding.

- **Take Notes**: Write down important points, definitions, and concepts as you study. Summarizing the material in your own words can help reinforce your understanding.
- **Create Flashcards**: Use flashcards to memorize key terms, laws, and procedures. Regularly review your flashcards to reinforce your memory.
- **Teach the Material**: Explain the concepts you've learned to someone else. Teaching the material to another person can help solidify your knowledge and highlight any gaps in your understanding.

4. Practice Regularly

Consistent practice is key to mastering the material and becoming comfortable with the exam format.

- **Answer Sample Questions**: At the end of each chapter in this book, practice answering the sample questions. Review the explanations to understand the reasoning behind each answer.
- **Simulate Exam Conditions**: Take the full-length practice exams under timed conditions to simulate the actual test environment. This will help you manage your time effectively during the real exam.
- **Review Mistakes**: Carefully review any mistakes you make on practice exams and sample questions. Understanding why you got a question wrong is crucial for improving your performance.

5. Stay Informed and Updated

Ensure you are aware of any updates or changes to the exam content and requirements.

- **Check Official Resources**: Regularly visit the New York Department of State's website for the latest information on the notary public exam, including any updates to laws and regulations.
- **Join Study Groups**: Connect with other aspiring notaries through study groups or online forums. Sharing knowledge and discussing difficult concepts can provide new insights and enhance your understanding.

6. Manage Exam Day Stress

Being well-prepared is the best way to reduce anxiety and boost your confidence on exam day.

- **Get a Good Night's Sleep**: Ensure you are well-rested before the exam. A good night's sleep will help you stay focused and alert.
- **Eat a Healthy Meal**: Have a nutritious meal before the exam to maintain your energy levels and concentration.
- **Arrive Early**: Plan to arrive at the exam location early to allow time for check-in and to get settled. Being rushed can increase stress levels.
- **Bring Necessary Materials**: Ensure you have all required materials, such as a valid photo ID and any other documents specified by the exam instructions.

Sample Study Schedule

Here's a sample study schedule to help you organize your preparation using this book:

Week 1-2: Focus on Notary Laws and Regulations
- Read and take notes on the New York Notary Public License Law
- Create flashcards for key laws and terms
- Answer sample questions related to laws and regulations in the book

Week 3-4: Study Duties and Responsibilities
- Review procedures for administering oaths, taking acknowledgments, and executing jurats
- Practice certifying copies and noting protests
- Take practice quizzes on notarial duties provided in the book

Week 5-6: Concentrate on Ethical Standards
- Study the principles of impartiality, confidentiality, and proper conduct
- Discuss ethical scenarios with study partners or groups
- Answer ethical standards practice questions from the book

Week 7-8: Master Procedures and Practices
- Learn the procedures for verifying identities and maintaining a notary journal
- Practice using a notary seal and performing remote notarizations
- Take full-length practice exams under timed conditions included in the book.

By following these preparation tips and strategies, you can approach the New York Notary Public Exam with confidence and increase your chances of success. Remember, consistent practice and a thorough understanding of the material are key to achieving your goal of becoming a notary public.

3.4 What to Do If You Don't Pass

While it's natural to feel disappointed if you don't pass the New York Notary Public Exam on your first attempt, it's important to view this as a learning opportunity. Many successful notaries have faced this challenge and gone on to achieve their certification. Here's a detailed guide on what steps to take if you don't pass the exam:

1. Review Your Results

The first step is to carefully review your exam results. Understanding where you went wrong can help you focus your study efforts more effectively.

- **Examine Your Score Report**: Look at the breakdown of your scores to identify specific areas where you struggled. This will help you pinpoint the topics that need more attention.

- **Identify Weak Areas**: Determine which sections (Notary Laws, Duties and Responsibilities, Ethical Standards, Procedures and Practices) had the most incorrect answers. This will guide your study focus.

2. Reflect on Your Preparation

Reflect on your study habits and preparation methods. Consider what worked well and what didn't.

- **Study Environment**: Evaluate whether your study environment was conducive to learning. Were there too many distractions? Did you have a dedicated, quiet place to study?
- **Study Techniques**: Assess the effectiveness of your study techniques. Did you use active learning methods like flashcards and teaching the material to someone else? Did you take regular practice exams?

3. Develop a Revised Study Plan

Create a new study plan that addresses the areas you need to improve and incorporates more effective study strategies.

- **Focused Study Sessions**: Allocate more time to the topics where you scored the lowest. Use the detailed explanations and sample questions in this book to deepen your understanding.
- **Active Learning**: Engage in active learning techniques, such as summarizing information in your own words, creating flashcards, and discussing topics with study partners.
- **Regular Practice**: Increase the frequency of practice exams and quizzes. Use the full-length practice exams included in this book to simulate the test environment and improve your time management skills.

4. Seek Additional Resources

If you feel that you need more help, consider using additional study resources to supplement your preparation.

- **Tutoring and Courses**: Enroll in a notary public preparation course or seek tutoring. These can provide structured learning and personalized guidance.
- **Online Forums and Study Groups**: Join online forums or study groups where you can ask questions, share insights, and get support from others who are also preparing for the exam.

5. Manage Stress and Stay Positive

Maintaining a positive mindset and managing stress is crucial for effective preparation and performance on your next attempt.

- **Stress Management Techniques**: Practice stress management techniques such as deep breathing exercises, meditation, and regular physical activity to keep your stress levels in check.
- **Positive Mindset**: Stay positive and remind yourself that many people do not pass the exam on their first try. Use this experience to strengthen your resolve and improve your preparation.

6. Register for the Exam Again

Once you feel more prepared, register to retake the exam. Ensure that you have reviewed all the necessary material and are confident in your knowledge and abilities.

- **Check Eligibility**: Verify that you are eligible to retake the exam and that you meet any required waiting periods between attempts.
- **Submit Application and Fee**: Complete the registration process and pay any applicable fees. Ensure all your information is accurate and up-to-date.

7. Exam Day Strategies

Approach your next exam attempt with a clear strategy to maximize your performance.

- **Review Key Concepts**: Do a quick review of key concepts and flashcards the day before the exam to keep the material fresh in your mind.

- **Rest and Nutrition**: Get a good night's sleep before the exam and eat a healthy meal to ensure you are physically and mentally prepared.
- **Time Management**: During the exam, manage your time effectively. Answer the questions you are confident about first, and then return to the more challenging ones.

Frequently Asked Questions (FAQs)

Q: How many times can I retake the New York Notary Public Exam? A: There is no limit to the number of times you can retake the exam. However, you must pay the exam fee for each attempt and adhere to any required waiting periods between attempts.

Q: How long do I have to wait before retaking the exam? A: The waiting period between exam attempts may vary. Check the New York Department of State's website for specific information on retake policies.

Q: Will my previous scores affect my new attempt? A: No, each exam attempt is scored independently. Your previous scores will not impact your new attempt.

Q: Can I get feedback on my specific answers? A: The New York Department of State does not typically provide detailed feedback on specific exam answers. However, your score report will highlight the areas where you need improvement.

Q: What should I focus on if I failed by a narrow margin? A: If you failed by a narrow margin, focus on reviewing the questions and topics where you lost the most points. Fine-tuning your knowledge in these areas can make a significant difference.

Not passing the New York Notary Public Exam on your first try can be a setback, but it is also an opportunity to learn and improve. By reviewing your results, reflecting on your preparation, and utilizing the comprehensive resources in this book, you can enhance your understanding and increase your chances of success on your next attempt.

4   RESPONSIBILITIES & DUTIES

4.1 Jurisdiction and Authority of Notaries

Understanding the jurisdiction and authority of a notary public is essential to performing your duties correctly and legally. This section will cover the scope of a notary's authority, the geographical limitations, and specific powers granted to notaries in New York.

Jurisdiction of Notaries

A notary public in New York has statewide jurisdiction. This means you are authorized to perform notarial acts anywhere within the boundaries of New York State. However, your commission is not valid outside of New York, and you cannot perform notarial acts in other states or countries under your New York commission.

- **Statewide Authority**: As a notary public, you can notarize documents anywhere in New York State, whether you are at home, at your office, or elsewhere within state lines.
- **Notary Commission**: Your authority as a notary public is granted by the New York Department of State, which issues your commission. This commission is your official authorization to act as a notary within the state.

Specific Powers of Notaries

Notaries public in New York have several specific powers, each with its own procedures and requirements. Understanding these powers ensures that you perform your duties accurately and legally.

1. **Acknowledgments**:
   - **Purpose**: To confirm that the signer of a document is who they claim to be and that they signed the document voluntarily.
   - **Procedure**: The signer must appear before the notary, provide satisfactory evidence of identity, and acknowledge that they signed the document.

2. **Jurats**:
   - **Purpose**: To administer an oath or affirmation and witness the signing of a document, typically an affidavit or deposition.
   - **Procedure**: The signer must swear or affirm the truthfulness of the document's content before the notary and then sign the document in the notary's presence.
3. **Oaths and Affirmations**:
   - **Purpose**: To formally affirm or swear to the truthfulness of a statement or document.
   - **Procedure**: The notary administers the oath or affirmation, and the signer acknowledges their understanding and agreement.
4. **Certifying Copies**:
   - **Purpose**: To attest that a copy of a document is a true and accurate reproduction of the original.
   - **Procedure**: The notary compares the copy with the original document and certifies its accuracy.
5. **Affidavits**:
   - **Purpose**: To certify a written statement made under oath.
   - **Procedure**: The affiant (person making the affidavit) appears before the notary, swears to the truthfulness of the statement, and signs the affidavit in the notary's presence.
6. **Noting Protests**:
   - **Purpose**: To formally note the dishonor of a negotiable instrument, such as a check or promissory note.
   - **Procedure**: The notary presents the instrument for payment or acceptance and notes the refusal. The notary then drafts a certificate of protest detailing the dishonor.

Geographical Limitations

While your commission allows you to perform notarial acts anywhere in New York State, you must be mindful of the following geographical limitations:

- **Out-of-State Restrictions**: You cannot perform notarial acts outside of New York State using your New York commission. Each state has its own requirements and regulations for notaries.

- **Cross-Border Situations**: If you are frequently involved in transactions that cross state lines, consider obtaining a notary commission in those states as well, if permitted.

Examples and Case Studies

Understanding the jurisdiction and authority of a notary public can be better grasped through real-world examples and case studies.

Example 1: Acknowledgment in Real Estate Transaction

- **Scenario**: Jane, a notary public, is asked to notarize a deed for a property sale in Albany, NY. The seller appears before Jane, provides a driver's license as identification, and acknowledges signing the deed.
- **Action**: Jane confirms the identity of the seller, witnesses the acknowledgment, and notarizes the deed, ensuring the transaction's legality.

Example 2: Jurat for an Affidavit

- **Scenario**: John, a notary public, is asked to notarize an affidavit for a legal proceeding in Buffalo, NY. The affiant appears before John, swears to the truthfulness of the affidavit's contents, and signs the document in John's presence.
- **Action**: John administers the oath, witnesses the signing, and notarizes the affidavit, ensuring the statement's validity for the court.

Example 3: Certifying a Copy of a Diploma

- **Scenario**: Maria, a notary public, is asked to certify a copy of a high school diploma for a college application in Rochester, NY. Maria compares the copy to the original diploma and certifies its accuracy.
- **Action**: Maria ensures that the copy is a true and accurate reproduction, notarizes the copy, and provides the certification needed for the application.

Common Pitfalls and How to Avoid Them

Being aware of common pitfalls can help you avoid mistakes and perform your duties more effectively:

- **Failing to Require Personal Appearance**: Always ensure that the signer appears before you in person. Notarizing a document without the signer present is illegal and can result in penalties.
- **Inadequate Identification**: Always verify the identity of the signer with satisfactory evidence, such as a government-issued ID. Never rely solely on personal familiarity or assumptions.
- **Incomplete Records**: Maintain thorough records of all notarial acts, including the date, type of act, and identification provided. This practice protects you in case of disputes or legal issues.

4.2 Key Duties and Liabilities

As a notary public in New York, you are entrusted with significant responsibilities that require adherence to strict legal and ethical standards. Understanding your key duties and the potential liabilities associated with your role is essential for performing your tasks effectively and maintaining public trust. This section outlines the core duties of a notary public, discusses common liabilities, and provides guidance on how to avoid pitfalls.

Key Duties of a Notary Public

1. **Administering Oaths and Affirmations**
   - **Purpose**: To legally bind a person to the truthfulness of their statements.
   - **Procedure**: The notary asks the individual to swear (oath) or affirm (affirmation) the truthfulness of the contents of a document. The notary must ensure the individual understands the significance of the oath or affirmation.
2. **Taking Acknowledgments**
   - **Purpose**: To confirm that the signer of a document is who they claim to be and that they signed the document voluntarily.
   - **Procedure**: The signer must appear before the notary, provide valid identification, and acknowledge that they

signed the document willingly. The notary verifies the identity of the signer and witnesses the acknowledgment.

3. **Executing Jurats**
   - **Purpose**: To certify that the statements in a document are sworn to be true by the signer.
   - **Procedure**: The signer appears before the notary, takes an oath or affirmation, and signs the document in the notary's presence. The notary then completes the jurat certificate.

4. **Certifying Copies**
   - **Purpose**: To attest that a copy of a document is a true and accurate reproduction of the original.
   - **Procedure**: The notary compares the copy with the original document and certifies its accuracy. The notary then signs and seals the certified copy.

5. **Noting Protests**
   - **Purpose**: To formally note the dishonor of a negotiable instrument, such as a check or promissory note.
   - **Procedure**: The notary presents the instrument for payment or acceptance and notes the refusal. The notary drafts a certificate of protest detailing the dishonor and the steps taken.

6. **Maintaining a Notary Journal**
   - **Purpose**: To keep a detailed record of all notarial acts performed.
   - **Procedure**: The notary records each notarial act in a journal, including the date, type of act, description of the document, and the signer's identification details. This record can be crucial for legal verification and accountability.

Liabilities of a Notary Public

As a notary public, you are liable for any mistakes or misconduct that occur during the performance of your duties. Understanding these liabilities and how to avoid them is crucial for protecting yourself and maintaining the integrity of your office.

1. **Civil Liability**
   - **Negligence**: Failing to perform notarial acts with the required level of care can lead to civil lawsuits. For example, notarizing a document without verifying the

identity of the signer can result in financial losses for third parties.

- o **Remedy**: To avoid negligence, always adhere to the proper procedures and verify the identity of all signers. Maintain accurate records and follow the laws governing notarial acts.

2. **Criminal Liability**
   - o **Fraud**: Engaging in fraudulent activities, such as forging signatures or knowingly notarizing false documents, can result in criminal charges.
   - o **Remedy**: Uphold the highest ethical standards and refuse to participate in any illegal or unethical activities. Report any suspicious requests to the appropriate authorities.

3. **Administrative Liability**
   - o **Violation of Notary Laws**: Failing to comply with the New York Notary Public License Law and other relevant statutes can lead to administrative penalties, including suspension or revocation of your notary commission.
   - o **Remedy**: Stay informed about the laws and regulations governing notaries in New York. Complete any required continuing education and renew your commission as needed.

Common Pitfalls and How to Avoid Them

Being aware of common pitfalls can help you avoid mistakes and perform your duties more effectively:

- **Failing to Require Personal Appearance**: Always ensure that the signer appears before you in person. Notarizing a document without the signer present is illegal and can result in penalties.
- **Inadequate Identification**: Always verify the identity of the signer with satisfactory evidence, such as a government-issued ID. Never rely solely on personal familiarity or assumptions.
- **Incomplete Records**: Maintain thorough records of all notarial acts, including the date, type of act, and identification provided. This practice protects you in case of disputes or legal issues.
- **Conflicts of Interest**: Avoid notarizing documents where you have a personal or financial interest. Notaries must remain impartial and avoid conflicts of interest to maintain public trust.

Case Studies and Real-World Examples

Understanding the practical application of notarial duties and liabilities can be enhanced through case studies and real-world examples.

Case Study 1: Negligence in Verifying Identity

- **Scenario**: A notary public in New York notarizes a property transfer document without properly verifying the identity of the signer. It is later discovered that the signer was an imposter, resulting in significant financial losses for the true property owner.
- **Outcome**: The notary faces a civil lawsuit for negligence, as well as potential disciplinary action from the New York Department of State.
- **Lesson**: Always verify the identity of signers using acceptable forms of identification to avoid negligence and protect all parties involved.

Case Study 2: Fraudulent Notarization

- **Scenario**: A notary public knowingly notarizes a false affidavit in exchange for a bribe. The fraudulent document is used in a legal proceeding, resulting in a miscarriage of justice.
- **Outcome**: The notary is charged with fraud and faces criminal penalties, including fines and imprisonment. Their notary commission is also revoked.
- **Lesson**: Uphold ethical standards and refuse to participate in any fraudulent activities. Report any attempts to bribe or coerce you into illegal actions.

Case Study 3: Incomplete Notary Journal

- **Scenario**: A notary public fails to maintain a complete notary journal, recording only some of the notarial acts performed. When a notarized document is later contested, there is no adequate record to verify the notarial act.
- **Outcome**: The notary is unable to provide evidence of the notarial act, leading to legal complications and potential liability.

- **Lesson**: Maintain a thorough and accurate notary journal for all notarial acts to ensure legal verification and protect yourself from liability.

4.3 Ethical Standards and Professional Conduct

As a notary public, you hold a position of public trust. Upholding ethical standards and maintaining professional conduct are paramount to ensuring the integrity of your role. This section explores the ethical obligations of a notary public, provides guidelines for professional behavior, and discusses how to handle ethical dilemmas.

Core Ethical Principles

1. **Impartiality**
   - **Definition**: A notary public must act as an impartial witness, without bias or favoritism towards any party involved in the transaction.
   - **Practice**: Avoid notarizing documents for close family members or where you have a personal or financial interest. Ensure that your actions do not favor one party over another.
2. **Integrity**
   - **Definition**: A notary public must act with honesty and integrity in all notarial acts.
   - **Practice**: Always perform your duties truthfully and accurately. Never engage in fraudulent activities or falsify documents.
3. **Confidentiality**
   - **Definition**: A notary public must maintain the confidentiality of all parties and documents involved in the notarial act.
   - **Practice**: Do not disclose any information about the notarization or the documents to unauthorized parties. Keep your notary journal and records secure.
4. **Competence**
   - **Definition**: A notary public must possess the necessary knowledge and skills to perform their duties effectively.
   - **Practice**: Stay informed about the latest laws and procedures related to notarization. Complete any required

continuing education and seek additional training if needed.

Professional Conduct Guidelines

1. **Maintain Accurate Records**
   - **Importance**: Keeping detailed and accurate records is essential for legal verification and accountability.
   - **Practice**: Use a notary journal to record each notarial act, including the date, type of act, document description, and signer's identification details.
2. **Proper Use of Notary Seal**
   - **Importance**: The notary seal is a critical tool that validates the notarial act.
   - **Practice**: Ensure your notary seal is secure and used only for legitimate notarizations. Never pre-stamp documents or leave your seal unattended.
3. **Charge Appropriate Fees**
   - **Importance**: Charging appropriate fees maintains transparency and trust.
   - **Practice**: Follow the fee schedule set by the New York Department of State. Provide a receipt for any fees collected and record the amount in your notary journal.
4. **Handle Ethical Dilemmas Appropriately**
   - **Importance**: Ethical dilemmas can arise in various situations, and handling them correctly is crucial for maintaining your integrity.
   - **Practice**: When faced with an ethical dilemma, consider the core ethical principles and seek advice if necessary. It is better to refuse a notarization than to compromise your ethical standards.

Case Studies and Real-World Examples

Understanding how to apply ethical principles in real-world scenarios can help you navigate complex situations effectively.

Case Study 1: Conflict of Interest

- **Scenario**: A notary public is asked to notarize a loan agreement for a close friend. The notary knows that their friend may not fully understand the terms of the agreement.
- **Action**: The notary explains the conflict of interest to their friend and recommends finding an impartial notary to handle the notarization.
- **Lesson**: Always avoid notarizing documents where a personal relationship could impair your impartiality.

Case Study 2: Handling Confidential Information

- **Scenario**: A notary public is presented with a sensitive legal document that contains confidential information. A third party requests details about the document.
- **Action**: The notary refuses to disclose any information about the document, citing confidentiality obligations.
- **Lesson**: Protect the privacy of the parties involved and maintain confidentiality at all times.

Case Study 3: Refusing a Notarization

- **Scenario**: A notary public suspects that a signer is under duress but cannot confirm it. The signer appears nervous and reluctant to answer questions.
- **Action**: The notary refuses to notarize the document, explaining that they cannot proceed if there is any doubt about the signer's willingness.
- **Lesson**: If you suspect coercion or duress, it is your duty to refuse the notarization to protect the integrity of the act and the parties involved.

Common Ethical Pitfalls and How to Avoid Them

Being aware of common ethical pitfalls can help you navigate your duties more effectively:

- **Notarizing Blank Documents**: Never notarize incomplete or blank documents. Ensure that all blanks are filled in and the document is complete before notarizing.

- **Conflicts of Interest**: Avoid notarizing documents where you have a personal or financial interest. Always remain impartial and unbiased.
- **Unauthorized Practice of Law**: Do not provide legal advice or interpret documents for signers. Refer them to a qualified attorney if they need legal assistance.

4.4 Prohibited Practices and Legal Boundaries

As a notary public, understanding the boundaries of your authority and the practices you are prohibited from engaging in is crucial. This section outlines the activities that notaries must avoid, the legal ramifications of overstepping these boundaries, and provides guidance on how to ensure compliance with New York State laws.

Prohibited Practices

1. **Unauthorized Practice of Law**
   - **Description**: Notaries public are not licensed to practice law. This includes giving legal advice, preparing legal documents, or representing someone in a legal matter.
   - **Examples**:
     - Drafting wills or contracts.
     - Advising signers on the legal implications of their documents.
     - Representing someone in court or legal proceedings.
   - **Consequences**: Engaging in the unauthorized practice of law can result in severe penalties, including fines, suspension or revocation of your notary commission, and potential criminal charges.
2. **Notarizing Documents without Personal Appearance**
   - **Description**: A notary public must not notarize a document unless the signer personally appears before them at the time of the notarization.
   - **Examples**:
     - Notarizing a document based on a phone call or email without seeing the signer in person.
     - Allowing someone else to sign on behalf of the original signer without proper authorization and documentation.

- o **Consequences**: Notarizing documents without the signer's personal appearance can lead to the invalidation of the notarized document, legal liability, and disciplinary actions against the notary.

3. **Notarizing Incomplete or Blank Documents**
   - o **Description**: A notary public must not notarize a document that contains blank spaces or is incomplete.
   - o **Examples**:
     - Notarizing a blank power of attorney form.
     - Notarizing a document with missing information that could be filled in later.
   - o **Consequences**: Notarizing incomplete or blank documents can facilitate fraud and result in serious legal consequences for both the notary and the parties involved.

4. **Conflict of Interest**
   - o **Description**: Notaries must avoid notarizing documents where they have a personal or financial interest. This ensures impartiality and prevents conflicts of interest.
   - o **Examples**:
     - Notarizing documents for immediate family members.
     - Notarizing documents in which the notary is named as a party or has a financial stake.
   - o **Consequences**: Engaging in notarizations where a conflict of interest exists can compromise the notary's impartiality and lead to legal challenges and penalties.

5. **Charging Excessive Fees**
   - o **Description**: Notaries in New York are limited to charging a maximum fee as prescribed by law for each notarial act.
   - o **Examples**:
     - Charging more than the allowable fee for notarizing a document.
     - Adding extra charges for services that are not authorized.
   - o **Consequences**: Overcharging for notarial services can result in fines, restitution to the affected parties, and disciplinary action against the notary.

6. **Improper Use of Notary Seal and Journal**
   - o **Description**: The notary seal and journal are critical tools that must be used properly and securely.
   - o **Examples**:

- Allowing others to use your notary seal.
- Pre-stamping documents before the notarization.
- Failing to record notarial acts in your journal.
  - **Consequences**: Misuse of the notary seal and journal can lead to fraud, legal liabilities, and the loss of your notary commission.

Legal Boundaries

Understanding and respecting the legal boundaries of your role as a notary public is essential to avoid overstepping your authority.

1. **Geographical Limitations**
   - **Description**: A New York notary public is authorized to perform notarial acts only within the state of New York.
   - **Guidelines**: Ensure all notarizations are conducted within state boundaries. If you frequently engage in cross-border transactions, understand the requirements of other states and seek additional commissions if necessary.
2. **Scope of Authority**
   - **Description**: Notaries have specific powers granted by law, including administering oaths, taking acknowledgments, and certifying copies. Do not perform acts outside these legally defined powers.
   - **Guidelines**: Familiarize yourself with the New York Notary Public License Law and adhere strictly to the duties and limitations it sets forth.

Case Studies and Real-World Examples

Examining real-world examples can help illustrate the importance of adhering to prohibited practices and legal boundaries.

Case Study 1: Unauthorized Practice of Law

- **Scenario**: A notary public drafts a will for a client, offering advice on estate planning.
- **Action**: The client later challenges the will in court, citing improper legal advice from the notary.
- **Outcome**: The notary faces legal action for unauthorized practice of law, resulting in fines and the loss of their notary commission.

- **Lesson**: Always refer clients to qualified attorneys for legal advice and document preparation.

Case Study 2: Notarizing without Personal Appearance

- **Scenario**: A notary notarizes a document for a friend who sends a scanned copy of their signature via email.
- **Action**: The document is later contested, and it is revealed that the signer never appeared before the notary.
- **Outcome**: The notarization is invalidated, and the notary faces disciplinary action for failing to follow proper procedures.
- **Lesson**: Never notarize a document without the signer personally appearing before you.

Case Study 3: Conflict of Interest

- **Scenario**: A notary notarizes a real estate document in which they have a financial interest.
- **Action**: The transaction is later disputed, and the notary's impartiality is called into question.
- **Outcome**: The notary faces legal challenges and penalties for violating conflict of interest rules.
- **Lesson**: Avoid notarizing documents where you have a personal or financial interest to maintain impartiality and trust.

Avoiding Common Pitfalls

Here are some practical tips to help you avoid common pitfalls and maintain compliance with New York State laws:

- **Stay Informed**: Regularly review the New York Notary Public License Law and stay updated on any changes or amendments.
- **Attend Training**: Participate in continuing education and training programs to enhance your knowledge and skills.
- **Use Checklists**: Develop checklists for each type of notarial act to ensure you follow all necessary steps and procedures.
- **Seek Guidance**: When in doubt, seek advice from experienced notaries, legal professionals, or the New York Department of State.

By understanding and adhering to the prohibited practices and legal boundaries outlined in this section, you can perform your duties with confidence and integrity. Maintaining compliance with New York State laws not only protects you from legal liabilities but also upholds the trust and reliability placed in you by the public.

5   EXECUTING NOTARIAL ACTS

5.1 Overview of Notarial Acts

As a notary public, you will perform various types of notarial acts, each with its own specific procedures and requirements. This section provides an overview of the different notarial acts, offering a foundation upon which the subsequent, more detailed sections will build. Understanding these acts is crucial to executing your duties effectively and maintaining the integrity of your role.

What Are Notarial Acts?

Notarial acts are official actions performed by a notary public as part of their authorized duties. These acts serve to authenticate documents, administer oaths, and perform other tasks that require an impartial and legally recognized witness. The primary purpose of notarial acts is to prevent fraud and ensure the validity and legality of documents.

Types of Notarial Acts

1. **Acknowledgments**
   - **Purpose**: To confirm that the signer of a document is who they claim to be and that they signed the document voluntarily.
   - **Common Uses**: Real estate transactions, legal agreements, powers of attorney.
2. **Jurats**
   - **Purpose**: To certify that the statements in a document are sworn to be true by the signer, who signs the document in the notary's presence.
   - **Common Uses**: Affidavits, depositions, sworn statements.

3. **Oaths and Affirmations**
   - **Purpose**: To administer a formal promise of truthfulness, either religious (oath) or secular (affirmation).
   - **Common Uses**: Court testimonies, affidavits, sworn statements.
4. **Certifying Copies**
   - **Purpose**: To attest that a copy of a document is a true and accurate reproduction of the original.
   - **Common Uses**: Educational certificates, identification documents, legal records.
5. **Noting Protests**
   - **Purpose**: To formally note the dishonor of a negotiable instrument, such as a check or promissory note.
   - **Common Uses**: Financial transactions, bank procedures.
6. **Proof of Execution**
   - **Purpose**: To verify that a document was signed in the presence of a witness, who then signs a statement before the notary attesting to this fact.
   - **Common Uses**: Legal agreements, contracts.
7. **Depositions**
   - **Purpose**: To record and certify sworn testimony outside of court.
   - **Common Uses**: Pre-trial procedures, legal proceedings.
8. **Loose Certificates**
   - **Purpose**: To provide a separate notarization certificate when there is no room on the document itself.
   - **Common Uses**: Attachments to legal documents, acknowledgments, jurats.

Step-by-Step Guides for Notarial Acts

Each type of notarial act requires a specific set of steps to be performed accurately and legally. The following sections will provide detailed, step-by-step guides for each notarial act, complete with visual aids to help you understand the process.

Common Mistakes and How to Correct Them

Even experienced notaries can make mistakes. Identifying common errors and knowing how to correct them is essential for maintaining the integrity of your notarial acts.

- **Mistake**: Not requiring personal appearance of the signer.
  - o **Correction**: Always ensure the signer is physically present before you at the time of notarization.
- **Mistake**: Incomplete or incorrect notary certificate.
  - o **Correction**: Double-check that all required elements (e.g., date, location, notary signature, seal) are correctly filled out.
- **Mistake**: Failing to properly identify the signer.
  - o **Correction**: Always ask for valid identification and ensure it matches the signer's information.

Visual Aids and Examples

Visual aids can be invaluable in understanding the proper execution of notarial acts. In the following sections, you will find diagrams, sample documents, and illustrations that demonstrate each step of the process. These visual aids will help you visualize the correct procedures and avoid common pitfalls.

5.2 Acknowledgments and Jurats

Acknowledgments and jurats are two of the most common notarial acts you will perform as a notary public. Each serves a distinct purpose and follows specific procedures. This section provides detailed step-by-step guides for executing acknowledgments and jurats, along with visual aids, common mistakes, and how to correct them.

Acknowledgments

Purpose: An acknowledgment is used to confirm that the person signing a document is who they claim to be and that they signed the document voluntarily. This notarial act is often required for documents that will be recorded in public records, such as real estate deeds and powers of attorney.

Step-by-Step Guide for Acknowledgments

1. **Personal Appearance**:
   - **Ensure the signer personally appears before you**.
   - **Check Identification**: Verify the signer's identity using a valid form of identification (e.g., driver's license, passport).
2. **Review the Document**:
   - **Examine the Document**: Ensure the document is complete and has no blank spaces. The notary should not offer legal advice or interpret the document.
   - **Confirm Details**: Verify that the name on the identification matches the name on the document.
3. **Signer Acknowledgment**:
   - **Ask the Signer**: Have the signer acknowledge that they signed the document voluntarily for its stated purposes.
   - **Record the Acknowledgment**: Note the details of the acknowledgment in your notary journal, including the date, type of document, and identification presented.
4. **Complete the Notarial Certificate**:
   - **Fill Out the Certificate**: Complete the acknowledgment certificate on the document. This includes the notary's signature, seal, date, and jurisdiction.
   - **Attach a Loose Certificate**: If there is no room on the document, attach a loose acknowledgment certificate.
5. **Affix the Notary Seal**:
   - **Seal the Document**: Affix your notary seal near your signature on the acknowledgment certificate. Ensure the seal impression is clear and legible.

Visual Aid for Acknowledgments

Include a diagram or image showing:

- The notary verifying identification.
- The signer acknowledging the document.
- The completed acknowledgment certificate with the notary's seal.

Common Mistakes and Corrections

- **Mistake**: Failing to personally appear before the signer.

- o **Correction**: Always require the signer to be physically present.
- **Mistake**: Not checking the signer's identification.
  - o **Correction**: Verify the identity of the signer using a valid ID.

Jurats

Purpose: A jurat is used to certify that the statements in a document are sworn to be true by the signer, who must sign the document in the notary's presence. This act is often required for affidavits and depositions.

Step-by-Step Guide for Jurats

1. **Personal Appearance**:
   - o **Ensure the signer personally appears before you**.
   - o **Check Identification**: Verify the signer's identity using a valid form of identification (e.g., driver's license, passport).
2. **Administer the Oath or Affirmation**:
   - o **Administer Oath/Affirmation**: Ask the signer to swear (oath) or affirm (affirmation) that the statements in the document are true.
   - o **Phrase**: Use a standard phrase, such as "Do you swear (or affirm) that the statements in this document are true, to the best of your knowledge?"
3. **Review the Document**:
   - o **Examine the Document**: Ensure the document is complete and has no blank spaces. The notary should not offer legal advice or interpret the document.
   - o **Confirm Details**: Verify that the name on the identification matches the name on the document.
4. **Signer's Signature**:
   - o **Witness the Signing**: Have the signer sign the document in your presence.
   - o **Record the Jurat**: Note the details of the jurat in your notary journal, including the date, type of document, and identification presented.
5. **Complete the Notarial Certificate**:
   - o **Fill Out the Certificate**: Complete the jurat certificate on the document. This includes the notary's signature, seal, date, and jurisdiction.
   - o **Attach a Loose Certificate**: If there is no room on the document, attach a loose jurat certificate.

6. **Affix the Notary Seal**:
    - **Seal the Document**: Affix your notary seal near your signature on the jurat certificate. Ensure the seal impression is clear and legible.

Visual Aid for Jurats

Include a diagram or image showing:
- The notary administering the oath or affirmation.
- The signer signing the document in the notary's presence.
- The completed jurat certificate with the notary's seal.

Common Mistakes and Corrections

- **Mistake**: Failing to administer the oath or affirmation.
    - **Correction**: Always administer the oath or affirmation as part of the jurat process.
- **Mistake**: Not witnessing the signer's signature.
    - **Correction**: Ensure the signer signs the document in your presence.

Acknowledgments and jurats are fundamental notarial acts that you will perform regularly. By understanding the specific procedures and requirements for each, you can ensure that these acts are executed correctly and legally. The visual aids and step-by-step guides provided in this section will help you navigate these processes with confidence, while the tips on avoiding common mistakes will enhance the integrity and accuracy of your notarial acts.

5.3 Oaths and Affirmations

Administering oaths and affirmations is a critical responsibility of a notary public. These notarial acts are used to formally affirm the truthfulness of statements in various legal and official documents. This section provides a detailed guide on how to properly administer oaths and affirmations, including step-by-step instructions, visual aids, common mistakes, and how to correct them.

Oaths and Affirmations

Purpose: Oaths and affirmations serve as a formal declaration of truthfulness. An oath involves a promise to a higher power, while an affirmation is a solemn declaration without religious connotations. Both are legally binding and carry the same weight in affirming the truthfulness of statements.

Step-by-Step Guide for Administering Oaths and Affirmations

1. **Personal Appearance**
   - **Ensure the signer personally appears before you**.
   - **Check Identification**: Verify the signer's identity using a valid form of identification (e.g., driver's license, passport).
2. **Explain the Process**
   - **Clarify the Difference**: Explain the difference between an oath and an affirmation to the signer and ask which they prefer to take.
   - **Inform the Signer**: Ensure the signer understands the seriousness and legal implications of taking an oath or affirmation.
3. **Administer the Oath or Affirmation**
   - **Standard Oath Phrase**: Ask the signer, "Do you swear that the statements in this document are true, so help you God?"
   - **Standard Affirmation Phrase**: Ask the signer, "Do you affirm that the statements in this document are true, under penalty of perjury?"
4. **Witness the Declaration**
   - **Observe the Response**: Ensure the signer responds affirmatively ("I do" or "Yes") to the oath or affirmation.
   - **Document the Act**: Record the details of the oath or affirmation in your notary journal, including the date, type of document, and identification presented.
5. **Complete the Notarial Certificate**
   - **Fill Out the Certificate**: Complete the notarial certificate on the document, noting the administration of the oath or affirmation.
   - **Attach a Loose Certificate**: If there is no room on the document, attach a loose certificate.

6. **Affix the Notary Seal**
   - **Seal the Document**: Affix your notary seal near your signature on the certificate. Ensure the seal impression is clear and legible.

Visual Aid for Oaths and Affirmations

Include a diagram or image showing:

- The notary administering the oath or affirmation.
- The signer making the declaration.
- The completed notarial certificate with the notary's seal.

Common Mistakes and Corrections

- **Mistake**: Not clarifying the difference between an oath and an affirmation.
   - **Correction**: Always explain the difference and ask the signer which they prefer.
- **Mistake**: Failing to witness the verbal declaration.
   - **Correction**: Ensure you hear the signer affirm or swear to the truthfulness of the statements.

Examples of Documents Requiring Oaths or Affirmations

1. **Affidavits**
   - **Scenario**: An affidavit is a written statement confirmed by oath or affirmation, used as evidence in court.
   - **Procedure**: Administer the oath or affirmation before the signer signs the affidavit in your presence.
2. **Depositions**
   - **Scenario**: A deposition is a witness's sworn out-of-court testimony, used in legal proceedings.
   - **Procedure**: Administer the oath or affirmation before the witness gives their testimony.
3. **Sworn Statements**
   - **Scenario**: Sworn statements are declarations made under oath or affirmation, used in various legal contexts.
   - **Procedure**: Administer the oath or affirmation before the signer signs the statement in your presence.

Ensuring Procedural Standards

1. **Verify Identity**
   - Always verify the identity of the person taking the oath or affirmation to ensure they are who they claim to be.
2. **Record Keeping**
   - Maintain accurate records in your notary journal, noting the details of each oath or affirmation administered.
3. **Legal Compliance**
   - Ensure compliance with New York State laws regarding the administration of oaths and affirmations. Stay informed about any updates or changes in the regulations.

Administering oaths and affirmations is a fundamental duty of a notary public. By following the proper procedures and maintaining high standards of practice, you can ensure the integrity and legality of these notarial acts. The visual aids and step-by-step guides provided in this section will help you navigate the process with confidence, while the tips on avoiding common mistakes will enhance the accuracy and reliability of your notarial services.

5.4 Handling Affidavits and Certifying Copies

Affidavits and certifying copies are common notarial acts that require precision and adherence to legal standards. This section provides detailed guides on how to properly handle affidavits and certify copies, including step-by-step instructions, visual aids, common mistakes, and how to correct them.

Affidavits

Purpose: An affidavit is a written statement made under oath or affirmation, used as evidence in legal proceedings. The notary's role is to administer the oath or affirmation and witness the signing of the document.

Step-by-Step Guide for Handling Affidavits

1. **Personal Appearance**
   - **Ensure the affiant personally appears before you**.
   - **Check Identification**: Verify the affiant's identity using a valid form of identification (e.g., driver's license, passport).
2. **Review the Affidavit**
   - **Examine the Document**: Ensure the affidavit is complete and has no blank spaces. The notary should not offer legal advice or interpret the document.
3. **Administer the Oath or Affirmation**
   - **Standard Oath Phrase**: Ask the affiant, "Do you swear that the statements in this affidavit are true, so help you God?"
   - **Standard Affirmation Phrase**: Ask the affiant, "Do you affirm that the statements in this affidavit are true, under penalty of perjury?"
4. **Witness the Signing**
   - **Observe the Signature**: Have the affiant sign the affidavit in your presence.
   - **Document the Act**: Record the details of the affidavit in your notary journal, including the date, type of document, and identification presented.
5. **Complete the Notarial Certificate**
   - **Fill Out the Certificate**: Complete the notarial certificate on the affidavit, noting the administration of the oath or affirmation.
   - **Attach a Loose Certificate**: If there is no room on the document, attach a loose certificate.
6. **Affix the Notary Seal**
   - **Seal the Document**: Affix your notary seal near your signature on the certificate. Ensure the seal impression is clear and legible.

Visual Aid for Affidavits

Include a diagram or image showing:

- The notary administering the oath or affirmation.
- The affiant signing the affidavit in the notary's presence.

- The completed notarial certificate with the notary's seal.

Common Mistakes and Corrections

- **Mistake**: Not administering the oath or affirmation.
  - **Correction**: Always administer the oath or affirmation as part of the affidavit process.
- **Mistake**: Not witnessing the affiant's signature.
  - **Correction**: Ensure the affiant signs the document in your presence.

Certifying Copies

Purpose: Certifying copies involves attesting that a copy of a document is a true and accurate reproduction of the original. This act is often required for legal and official purposes where original documents cannot be provided.

Step-by-Step Guide for Certifying Copies

1. **Personal Appearance**
   - **Ensure the requester personally appears before you**.
   - **Check Identification**: Verify the requester's identity using a valid form of identification (e.g., driver's license, passport).
2. **Examine the Original Document**
   - **Review the Original**: Ensure the original document is complete and not altered or damaged.
   - **Confirm Details**: Compare the original document with the copy to ensure accuracy.
3. **Certify the Copy**
   - **Statement of Certification**: Write or stamp a statement on the copy certifying that it is a true and accurate reproduction of the original.
   - **Include Details**: The statement should include the notary's signature, seal, the date, and a declaration such as "I certify that this is a true and accurate copy of the original document."

4. **Record the Act**
   - **Document the Certification**: Record the details of the certification in your notary journal, including the date, type of document, and identification presented.
5. **Affix the Notary Seal**
   - **Seal the Document**: Affix your notary seal near your certification statement. Ensure the seal impression is clear and legible.

Visual Aid for Certifying Copies

Include a diagram or image showing:

- The notary comparing the original document with the copy.
- The notary writing or stamping the certification statement on the copy.
- The completed certification statement with the notary's seal.

Common Mistakes and Corrections

- **Mistake**: Certifying a copy without comparing it to the original.
   - **Correction**: Always compare the copy with the original document to ensure accuracy.
- **Mistake**: Incomplete certification statement.
   - **Correction**: Ensure the certification statement includes all necessary details, such as the notary's signature, seal, date, and declaration.

Examples of Documents Requiring Affidavits and Certified Copies

1. **Legal Proceedings**
   - **Affidavits**: Used as evidence in court cases, requiring the affiant to swear to the truthfulness of their statements.
   - **Certified Copies**: Providing certified copies of legal documents, such as court orders or judgments, when originals cannot be submitted.
2. **Business Transactions**
   - **Affidavits**: Used in business transactions to affirm the truthfulness of statements or claims.
   - **Certified Copies**: Certifying copies of business licenses, permits, or contracts for official purposes.

3. **Personal Matters**
    - **Affidavits**: Used in personal matters, such as affirming residency, marital status, or other personal claims.
    - **Certified Copies**: Certifying copies of personal documents, such as birth certificates, diplomas, or identification cards.

Conclusion

Handling affidavits and certifying copies are integral parts of a notary public's duties. By following the proper procedures and maintaining high standards of practice, you can ensure the accuracy and legality of these notarial acts. The visual aids and step-by-step guides provided in this section will help you navigate the process with confidence, while the tips on avoiding common mistakes will enhance the reliability and integrity of your notarial services.

5.5 Noting Protests and Proof of Execution

Noting protests and providing proof of execution are less common but equally important notarial acts. These tasks involve certifying certain financial transactions and verifying the execution of documents in the presence of witnesses. This section provides detailed guides on how to properly note protests and provide proof of execution, including step-by-step instructions, visual aids, common mistakes, and how to correct them.

Noting Protests

Purpose: A protest is a formal declaration made by a notary public when a negotiable instrument, such as a check or promissory note, is dishonored. This act is primarily used in financial and banking contexts to certify that payment has been refused.

Step-by-Step Guide for Noting Protests

1. **Personal Appearance**
    - **Ensure the holder of the negotiable instrument personally appears before you.**
    - **Check Identification**: Verify the holder's identity using a valid form of identification (e.g., driver's license, passport).

2. **Examine the Instrument**
   - **Review the Negotiable Instrument**: Ensure the instrument is complete and check for any endorsements or alterations.
3. **Present the Instrument**
   - **Attempt to Collect Payment**: Present the instrument to the party responsible for payment and formally request payment.
   - **Record the Refusal**: Note the refusal to pay, including the date, time, and reason for dishonor (e.g., insufficient funds, signature mismatch).
4. **Prepare the Certificate of Protest**
   - **Document Details**: Draft a certificate of protest, including details of the instrument, the parties involved, the date of presentation, and the reason for refusal.
   - **Sign and Seal**: Sign the certificate and affix your notary seal.
5. **Record the Act**
   - **Document the Protest**: Record the details of the protest in your notary journal, including the date, type of instrument, parties involved, and reason for dishonor.

Visual Aid for Noting Protests

Include a diagram or image showing:

- The notary presenting the negotiable instrument for payment.
- The recording of the refusal to pay.
- The completed certificate of protest with the notary's seal.

Common Mistakes and Corrections

- **Mistake**: Failing to present the instrument properly.
  - **Correction**: Ensure the instrument is presented to the responsible party and the refusal is documented accurately.
- **Mistake**: Incomplete certificate of protest.
  - **Correction**: Include all necessary details in the certificate, such as the date, parties involved, and reason for refusal.

Proof of Execution

Purpose: Proof of execution is used to verify that a document was signed in the presence of a witness, who then signs a statement before the notary attesting to this fact. This act is often required for legal documents to confirm their authenticity.

Step-by-Step Guide for Proof of Execution

1. **Personal Appearance**
   - **Ensure the witness personally appears before you**.
   - **Check Identification**: Verify the witness's identity using a valid form of identification (e.g., driver's license, passport).
2. **Review the Document**
   - **Examine the Document**: Ensure the document is complete and has no blank spaces.
3. **Witness Statement**
   - **Obtain Witness Statement**: Have the witness state that they saw the principal sign the document.
   - **Document the Statement**: Record the witness's statement in your notary journal, including the date, type of document, and identification presented.
4. **Witness Signature**
   - **Witness Signs**: Have the witness sign the document or a separate proof of execution statement in your presence.
5. **Complete the Notarial Certificate**
   - **Fill Out the Certificate**: Complete the proof of execution certificate on the document, noting the witness's statement and signature.
   - **Attach a Loose Certificate**: If there is no room on the document, attach a loose certificate.
6. **Affix the Notary Seal**
   - **Seal the Document**: Affix your notary seal near your signature on the certificate. Ensure the seal impression is clear and legible.

Visual Aid for Proof of Execution
Include a diagram or image shwwing:
- The notary obtaining the witness's statement.
- The witness signing the document in the notary's presence.

- The completed proof of execution certificate with the notary's seal.

Common Mistakes and Corrections

- **Mistake**: Not verifying the identity of the witness.
  - o **Correction**: Always check the witness's identification to ensure they are who they claim to be.
- **Mistake**: Incomplete proof of execution statement.
  - o **Correction**: Ensure the statement includes all necessary details, such as the witness's statement, signature, and your notary seal.

Examples of Documents Requiring Protests and Proof of Execution

1. **Financial Transactions**
   - o **Protests**: Used when negotiable instruments like checks or promissory notes are dishonored. The protest provides legal proof of the dishonor.
   - o **Example**: A check is returned for insufficient funds, and the holder requests a notary to note the protest.
2. **Legal Agreements**
   - o **Proof of Execution**: Used to verify that a document was signed in the presence of a witness, ensuring its authenticity.
   - o **Example**: A real estate deed requires a witness to confirm the principal's signature.
3. **Contracts**
   - o **Proof of Execution**: Provides verification that the parties involved in a contract signed it in the presence of a witness.
   - o **Example**: A business contract where a witness needs to attest to the signing parties' identities and the document's execution.

Noting protests and providing proof of execution are specialized notarial acts that require careful attention to detail and adherence to legal standards. By following the proper procedures and maintaining high standards of practice, you can ensure the accuracy and legality of these acts. The visual aids and step-by-step guides provided in this section will help you navigate the process with confidence, while the tips on avoiding common mistakes will enhance the reliability and integrity of your notarial services.

5.6 Managing Depositions and Loose Certificates

Managing depositions and issuing loose certificates are crucial notarial acts that require meticulous attention to detail and a thorough understanding of legal requirements. This section provides detailed guides on how to handle depositions and issue loose certificates, including step-by-step instructions, visual aids, common mistakes, and how to correct them.

Depositions

Purpose: A deposition is a sworn, out-of-court testimony used in legal proceedings. The notary's role is to administer the oath or affirmation to the deponent (witness) and document the testimony accurately.

Step-by-Step Guide for Managing Depositions

1. **Personal Appearance**
   - **Ensure the deponent personally appears before you**.
   - **Check Identification**: Verify the deponent's identity using a valid form of identification (e.g., driver's license, passport).
2. **Administer the Oath or Affirmation**
   - **Standard Oath Phrase**: Ask the deponent, "Do you swear that the testimony you are about to give is the truth, the whole truth, and nothing but the truth, so help you God?"
   - **Standard Affirmation Phrase**: Ask the deponent, "Do you affirm that the testimony you are about to give is the truth, the whole truth, and nothing but the truth, under penalty of perjury?"
3. **Record the Testimony**
   - **Accurate Documentation**: Ensure the deposition is recorded accurately, either by a court reporter or using a reliable recording device.
   - **Verbal Agreement**: Have the deponent confirm verbally that the testimony recorded is accurate and complete.

4. **Review and Sign**
    o   **Review the Transcript**: If a transcript is created, have the deponent review it for accuracy.
    o   **Deponent Signature**: Have the deponent sign the transcript to confirm its accuracy.
5. **Complete the Notarial Certificate**
    o   **Fill Out the Certificate**: Complete the notarial certificate on the deposition, noting the administration of the oath or affirmation.
    o   **Attach a Loose Certificate**: If there is no room on the document, attach a loose certificate.
6. **Affix the Notary Seal**
    o   **Seal the Document**: Affix your notary seal near your signature on the certificate. Ensure the seal impression is clear and legible.

Visual Aid for Depositions

Include a diagram or image showing:

- The notary administering the oath or affirmation to the deponent.
- The recording of the testimony.
- The completed notarial certificate with the notary's seal.

Common Mistakes and Corrections

- **Mistake**: Not administering the oath or affirmation.
    o   **Correction**: Always administer the oath or affirmation as part of the deposition process.
- **Mistake**: Inaccurate documentation of the testimony.
    o   **Correction**: Ensure the testimony is recorded accurately and reviewed by the deponent.

Loose Certificates

Purpose: A loose certificate is used when there is no room on the document itself for the notarial certificate. It serves as an attached page that contains the notarial wording, notary's signature, and seal.

Step-by-Step Guide for Issuing Loose Certificates

1. **Personal Appearance**
   - **Ensure the signer personally appears before you**.
   - **Check Identification**: Verify the signer's identity using a valid form of identification (e.g., driver's license, passport).
2. **Review the Document**
   - **Examine the Document**: Ensure the document is complete and has no blank spaces.
3. **Complete the Loose Certificate**
   - **Fill Out the Certificate**: Complete the notarial certificate on the loose certificate, noting the type of notarial act performed.
   - **Attach the Certificate**: Securely attach the loose certificate to the document it pertains to. Use a staple or other permanent method to prevent separation.
4. **Affix the Notary Seal**
   - **Seal the Loose Certificate**: Affix your notary seal on the loose certificate. Ensure the seal impression is clear and legible.
5. **Record the Act**
   - **Document the Notarization**: Record the details of the notarization in your notary journal, including the date, type of document, and identification presented.

Visual Aid for Loose Certificates

Include a diagram or image showing:

- The notary completing the loose certificate.
- The attachment of the loose certificate to the original document.
- The completed loose certificate with the notary's seal.

Common Mistakes and Corrections

- **Mistake**: Not securely attaching the loose certificate to the document.
  - **Correction**: Use a staple or other permanent method to attach the loose certificate securely to the document.
- **Mistake**: Incomplete or incorrect loose certificate.

- o **Correction**: Ensure the loose certificate includes all necessary details, such as the type of notarial act, date, notary's signature, and seal.

Examples of Situations Requiring Depositions and Loose Certificates

1. **Legal Proceedings**
   - o **Depositions**: Used to gather sworn testimony from witnesses before a trial. The notary ensures the testimony is given under oath and documented accurately.
   - o **Example**: A witness's deposition is taken for a civil lawsuit.
2. **Business Transactions**
   - o **Loose Certificates**: Used when notarizing documents that lack space for the notarial certificate. The loose certificate is attached to ensure the notarization is valid.
   - o **Example**: A corporate resolution requires a loose certificate due to space constraints.
3. **Personal Matters**
   - o **Depositions**: Used in personal legal matters, such as family law cases, where witness testimony is required.
   - o **Loose Certificates**: Used for personal documents, such as affidavits or declarations, that need additional notarization space.
   - o **Example**: A family member's deposition is taken for a probate case.

Managing depositions and issuing loose certificates are specialized notarial acts that require careful attention to detail and adherence to legal standards. By following the proper procedures and maintaining high standards of practice, you can ensure the accuracy and legality of these acts. The visual aids and step-by-step guides provided in this section will help you navigate the process with confidence, while the tips on avoiding common mistakes will enhance the reliability and integrity of your notarial services.

6 REMOTE NOTARIZATION AND TECHNOLOGY

6.1 Introduction to Remote Notarization

Remote notarization has revolutionized the traditional practice of notarization by leveraging technology to facilitate the notarization process from virtually anywhere. This chapter introduces the fundamentals of remote notarization, outlining its purpose, advantages, and relevance in the modern digital era.

What is Remote Notarization?

Remote notarization, also known as online or electronic notarization, is a process by which a notary public performs notarial acts using audio-visual technology to communicate with the signer in real-time. Unlike traditional notarization, which requires physical presence, remote notarization allows the notary and the signer to be in different locations while maintaining the integrity and security of the notarization process.

Key elements of remote notarization include:

1. **Real-Time Communication:** The notary and signer interact via a secure audio-visual platform.
2. **Identity Verification:** The signer's identity is authenticated through credential analysis and identity proofing methods.
3. **Electronic Signatures:** Both the signer and notary use electronic signatures to execute the document.
4. **Digital Record-Keeping:** The entire notarization session is recorded and stored as part of compliance requirements.

Evolution and Adoption of Remote Notarization

The concept of remote notarization gained momentum with advancements in technology and the increasing need for convenient and efficient notarization solutions. Several factors contributed to its adoption:

- **Legislative Changes:** States across the U.S., including New York, have enacted laws to permit and regulate remote notarization.
- **Technological Innovation:** Secure platforms for audio-visual communication, digital signatures, and identity verification have made remote notarization practical and reliable.
- **Pandemic Response:** During the COVID-19 pandemic, remote notarization emerged as a vital tool for ensuring continuity in notarization services while adhering to social distancing guidelines.

Benefits of Remote Notarization

Remote notarization offers numerous advantages for notaries, signers, and businesses alike:

1. **Convenience:** Signers can complete notarization from the comfort of their homes or offices, eliminating the need for travel.
2. **Accessibility:** Remote notarization makes services available to individuals in rural or remote areas who may not have easy access to a traditional notary.
3. **Efficiency:** The process is faster and reduces delays associated with scheduling in-person meetings.
4. **Security:** Advanced technology ensures secure identity verification and document integrity.
5. **Compliance:** Digital records of notarization sessions provide robust documentation for legal and regulatory purposes.

Key Applications of Remote Notarization

Remote notarization is applicable in various scenarios, including:

- **Real Estate Transactions:** Facilitating the signing of mortgage documents, deeds, and other real estate contracts.
- **Financial Agreements:** Streamlining the notarization of loan agreements, contracts, and other financial documents.
- **Legal Proceedings:** Enabling remote affidavits, depositions, and powers of attorney.
- **Personal Documents:** Simplifying the notarization of wills, healthcare directives, and consent forms.

Challenges and Considerations

While remote notarization offers significant benefits, it also presents challenges that require careful consideration:

- **Technology Requirements:** Both notaries and signers must have access to reliable internet, compatible devices, and secure platforms.
- **Regulatory Compliance:** Notaries must adhere to state-specific laws and regulations governing remote notarization.
- **Training and Familiarity:** Notaries need proper training to effectively use remote notarization technology.
- **Privacy Concerns:** Ensuring the confidentiality of sensitive documents and personal information is critical.

Remote notarization represents a transformative development in the field of notarization, offering unparalleled convenience, efficiency, and security.

6.2 Legal Requirements and Procedures

Understanding the legal framework and procedures for remote notarization is essential for notaries to ensure compliance and provide valid services. This chapter outlines the key legal requirements and step-by-step procedures to conduct remote notarizations in accordance with state and federal regulations.

Legal Foundations of Remote Notarization

Remote notarization is governed by a combination of state laws, federal guidelines, and industry standards. The specific legal requirements may vary by jurisdiction, but common elements include:

1. **Authorization by State Law:** Notaries must verify that their state permits remote notarization and adhere to the specific regulations outlined.
2. **Identity Proofing and Credential Analysis:** These processes involve verifying the signer's identity through government-issued identification and additional security checks.
3. **Electronic Notarization Platforms:** Notaries must use state-approved platforms that meet stringent security and privacy standards.
4. **Record-Keeping Requirements:** States often mandate the retention of electronic records, including audio-visual recordings and digital certificates.
5. **Registration and Certification:** Notaries may need to register with their state to perform remote notarizations and complete any required training or certification.

Step-by-Step Procedures for Remote Notarization

Conducting a remote notarization involves the following steps:

1. **Preparation:**
   - Verify the legality of remote notarization in your jurisdiction.
   - Select a compliant electronic notarization platform.
   - Ensure you and the signer have the necessary technology, including internet access and a webcam-enabled device.
2. **Identity Verification:**
   - Request the signer to present a government-issued ID.
   - Utilize the platform's credential analysis and identity proofing tools to authenticate the signer.
3. **Document Review:**
   - Ensure the document is complete and free of blank spaces.

- o Confirm that the signer understands the content and purpose of the document.
4. **Audio-Visual Communication:**
   - o Initiate a secure audio-visual session with the signer.
   - o Maintain clear communication throughout the process to verify the signer's willingness and competence.
5. **Execution of the Document:**
   - o Guide the signer in applying their electronic signature to the document.
   - o Affix your electronic signature and notarial seal, as required.
6. **Record the Session:**
   - o Capture and store a recording of the notarization session, as mandated by state law.
   - o Log the details of the notarization in your electronic notary journal.
7. **Finalize and Deliver:**
   - o Provide a copy of the notarized document to the signer.
   - o Retain all necessary records for the required retention period.

Common Pitfalls and How to Avoid Them

1. **Inadequate Identity Verification:** Always use approved methods to authenticate the signer's identity.
2. **Technical Failures:** Test the platform and internet connection beforehand to avoid disruptions.
3. **Non-Compliance with State Laws:** Stay updated on legal requirements and any changes in remote notarization regulations.
4. **Improper Record-Keeping:** Maintain thorough records, including session recordings and journal entries, to ensure compliance.

By adhering to the legal requirements and following established procedures, notaries can conduct remote notarizations confidently and competently. This ensures the validity of their notarial acts and enhances trust in their services, paving the way for a secure and efficient notarization process in the digital age.

6.3 Credential Analysis and Identity Proofing

Credential analysis and identity proofing are fundamental components of remote notarization, ensuring that the signer's identity is verified with accuracy and security. This chapter delves into the processes, technologies, and best practices that enable notaries to authenticate identities effectively in a remote environment.

Importance of Credential Analysis and Identity Proofing

In remote notarization, verifying the identity of signers is critical to maintaining the integrity of the notarial act. Credential analysis and identity proofing:

1. **Prevent Fraud:** Ensure that only authorized individuals can execute documents.
2. **Enhance Security:** Leverage advanced technologies to minimize the risk of identity theft and forgery.
3. **Build Trust:** Provide assurance to all parties involved in the transaction that the document is legitimate.

Credential Analysis

Credential analysis involves verifying the authenticity of a government-issued ID or other acceptable forms of identification. This process is typically performed through automated systems integrated into electronic notarization platforms.

Key Steps in Credential Analysis:

1. **Capture the ID:** The signer uploads a clear, high-resolution image of their identification document.
2. **Validate Authenticity:** The platform checks for security features, such as holograms, watermarks, and microtext, to confirm the document's legitimacy.
3. **Extract Information:** Relevant details, such as the signer's name, date of birth, and ID number, are extracted for verification.
4. **Cross-Check Data:** The system cross-references the extracted information with external databases to confirm accuracy.

Identity Proofing

Identity proofing complements credential analysis by ensuring that the individual presenting the ID is its rightful owner. This process typically involves multi-factor authentication.

Methods of Identity Proofing:

1. **Knowledge-Based Authentication (KBA):**
   - The signer answers a series of personal questions based on information from public and private databases.
   - Questions may include details about past addresses, financial transactions, or other verifiable data.

2. **Biometric Verification:**
    o The signer's biometric data, such as facial recognition or fingerprint scanning, is compared against the ID photo.
    o Biometric tools enhance security by adding an additional layer of verification.
3. **One-Time Passcodes (OTP):**
    o A unique code is sent to the signer's registered phone number or email address.
    o The signer enters the code into the notarization platform to complete the authentication process.

Challenges in Credential Analysis and Identity Proofing
1. **Technical Limitations:** Low-quality images or outdated hardware may affect the accuracy of ID analysis.
2. **User Errors:** Signers may struggle with the technology, such as incorrectly capturing ID images or failing KBA questions.
3. **Privacy Concerns:** Storing sensitive personal information requires strict adherence to data protection laws and best practices.

Best Practices for Notaries
1. **Use Reliable Platforms:** Choose notarization platforms with robust credential analysis and identity proofing capabilities.
2. **Educate Signers:** Provide clear instructions on how to prepare their ID and complete the identity verification process.
3. **Stay Updated:** Keep abreast of advancements in identity verification technologies and adapt to new tools as needed.
4. **Ensure Compliance:** Verify that all processes align with state and federal regulations regarding identity proofing and data security.

Credential analysis and identity proofing are essential to the success and security of remote notarization. By leveraging advanced technologies and following best practices, notaries can uphold the highest standards of trust and authenticity, ensuring that remote notarizations are both reliable and secure.

6.4 Record Keeping and Compliance

Record keeping and compliance are vital aspects of remote notarization, ensuring that all notarial acts are properly documented and adhere to legal and regulatory requirements. This chapter explores the importance of accurate record keeping, outlines best practices, and highlights key compliance considerations for notaries.

The Importance of Record Keeping
Effective record keeping serves multiple purposes in the context of remote notarization:
1. **Legal Compliance:** Many jurisdictions require notaries to maintain detailed records of their notarial acts, including audio-visual recordings and journal entries.
2. **Fraud Prevention:** Comprehensive records provide evidence that can deter fraudulent claims or disputes.
3. **Accountability:** Accurate documentation ensures that notaries can demonstrate adherence to legal and ethical standards.
4. **Professional Integrity:** Maintaining detailed records enhances the credibility and reliability of notarial services.

Key Elements of Record Keeping
To ensure compliance, notaries must focus on the following elements:
1. **Electronic Notary Journal:**
   - Record details of each notarial act, including the date, time, type of act, and signer's information.
   - Note the methods used for identity verification, such as credential analysis and identity proofing.
2. **Audio-Visual Recordings:**
   - Capture the entire notarization session, including interactions with the signer and the execution of the document.
   - Store recordings securely for the retention period specified by state law.
3. **Digital Certificates and Seals:**
   - Ensure that electronic signatures and seals meet legal standards for authenticity and security.
   - Retain copies of digital certificates used in remote notarization.
4. **Document Retention:**
   - Retain electronic copies of notarized documents in a secure, accessible format.
   - Follow state-specific guidelines for the retention period, typically ranging from 5 to 10 years.

Best Practices for Record Keeping
1. **Use Compliant Platforms:** Select electronic notarization platforms that automatically generate and store required records in a secure environment.

2. **Organize Records:** Develop a systematic approach to organize journal entries, recordings, and documents for easy retrieval.
3. **Secure Storage:** Protect records from unauthorized access, data breaches, and loss through encryption and regular backups.
4. **Regular Audits:** Periodically review records to ensure accuracy and completeness, addressing any discrepancies promptly.

Compliance Considerations

1. **Adherence to State Laws:** Understand and follow the specific record-keeping and compliance requirements in your jurisdiction.
2. **Privacy and Data Protection:** Ensure that all records, particularly those containing sensitive personal information, comply with data protection laws, such as GDPR or CCPA.
3. **Training and Certification:** Stay updated on legal and technological changes through continuing education and training programs.
4. **Reporting Obligations:** Be prepared to provide records to regulatory authorities or parties involved in the notarization if required.

Common Challenges and Solutions

1. **Technical Issues:** Use reliable and user-friendly platforms to minimize technical disruptions during record keeping.
2. **Storage Limitations:** Invest in scalable cloud storage solutions to accommodate growing record-keeping needs.
3. **Compliance Gaps:** Regularly review state laws and regulations to ensure ongoing compliance with record-keeping standards.

Record keeping and compliance are foundational to the success and legitimacy of remote notarization. By adopting best practices and leveraging secure technologies, notaries can fulfill their legal obligations, protect against fraud, and uphold the highest standards of professionalism. Through meticulous documentation, notaries contribute to the trust and reliability essential to the remote notarization process.

6.5 Remote Notarization Fees and Registration

The implementation of remote notarization introduces specific considerations for fees and registration processes. This chapter explores the fee structures associated with remote notarization, outlines registration requirements for notaries, and highlights best practices for managing these elements effectively.

Remote Notarization Fee Structures

Fees for remote notarization are regulated by state laws and may vary based on jurisdiction. Notaries must ensure their fees are compliant with local regulations while reflecting the added value of remote services.

1. **Maximum Allowable Fees:**
   - Many states set a cap on the fees that notaries can charge for remote notarization.
   - Verify the maximum allowable fee in your state and avoid exceeding this limit.

2. **Additional Technology Fees:**
   - Some jurisdictions permit notaries to charge additional fees to cover the cost of remote notarization technology.
   - Clearly disclose any technology-related fees to the signer before initiating the notarization.

3. **Transparency in Pricing:**
   - Provide a detailed breakdown of fees, including notarization and technology charges.
   - Issue receipts for all payments to maintain transparency and accountability.

Registration Requirements for Remote Notaries

To perform remote notarizations, notaries must often complete specific registration steps with their state's commissioning authority. These requirements ensure that notaries are equipped to provide secure and compliant remote services.

1. **State Authorization:**
   - Verify that your state permits remote notarization and determine the registration requirements.
   - Complete any necessary applications or forms to receive authorization.

2. **Training and Certification:**
   - Many states require notaries to complete training courses or pass an exam focused on remote notarization laws and practices.
   - Obtain a certificate of completion to demonstrate your preparedness.

3. **Technology Platform Approval:**
   - Use a state-approved electronic notarization platform that meets security and compliance standards.
   - Provide documentation of your chosen platform during the registration process, if required.

4. **Updated Commission Information:**
    o   Ensure your notary commission includes authorization for remote notarization.
    o   Update your commission details with the state to reflect this capability.

Best Practices for Managing Fees and Registration

1. **Stay Informed:** Regularly review state laws and updates regarding fee structures and registration requirements.
2. **Maintain Accurate Records:** Keep detailed records of fees charged, payments received, and registration documentation.
3. **Communicate Clearly:** Explain all fees and registration-related requirements to signers to ensure mutual understanding.
4. **Audit and Review:** Periodically review your fee schedule and registration status to ensure ongoing compliance with state regulations.

Common Challenges and Solutions

1. **Fee Disputes:**
    o   Solution: Provide clear, upfront explanations of fees and obtain written consent from signers before proceeding.
2. **Registration Delays:**
    o   Solution: Begin the registration process early and follow up with state authorities as needed to avoid interruptions in service.
3. **Changing Regulations:**
    o   Solution: Stay updated on legislative changes through professional organizations, state resources, or continuing education programs.

Conclusion

Effective management of fees and registration processes is essential for the success of remote notarization services. By adhering to state regulations, maintaining transparency

6.6 Security Protocols for AV Technology

To excel in providing remote notarization services, notaries must adopt a set of best practices that ensure efficiency, compliance, and professionalism. This chapter offers actionable insights and strategies for delivering high-quality remote notarization experiences.

Key Components of Best Practices

1. **Client Communication:**
   - Clearly explain the remote notarization process to clients, including technology requirements and identity verification steps.
   - Provide step-by-step guidance to help clients prepare their documents and technology for the session.
2. **Technology Mastery:**
   - Familiarize yourself with the remote notarization platform's features and functionality.
   - Conduct test runs to ensure smooth operation during actual notarization sessions.
3. **Compliance Awareness:**
   - Stay updated on state-specific laws and regulations governing remote notarization.
   - Ensure all processes, from identity verification to record keeping, align with legal requirements.
4. **Professionalism:**
   - Maintain a professional demeanor during video sessions to instill confidence in clients.
   - Dress appropriately and ensure a clutter-free background to create a professional virtual setting.
5. **Secure Data Management:**
   - Use encryption and other security measures to protect sensitive information during and after notarization sessions.
   - Avoid storing unnecessary personal data to minimize risks of data breaches.
6. **Preparation and Punctuality:**
   - Review documents in advance to ensure accuracy and completeness.
   - Be punctual and respect the client's time by adhering to scheduled appointments.

Common Challenges and Solutions
1. **Technical Glitches:**
   - Solution: Test equipment and internet connections beforehand. Keep a backup device ready for emergencies.

2. **Client Confusion:**
   - Solution: Offer clear, concise instructions and provide FAQs or tutorials to help clients understand the process.
3. **Regulatory Ambiguity:**
   - Solution: Regularly consult state authorities or legal advisors to stay informed about regulatory changes.
4. **Privacy Concerns:**
   - Solution: Use platforms that comply with data protection standards and educate clients on how their information will be handled.

Enhancing Client Experience
1. **Personalization:**
   - Address clients by name and create a welcoming atmosphere during the session.
2. **Transparency:**
   - Explain each step of the notarization process and answer any questions clients may have.
3. **Follow-Up:**
   - Provide clients with a copy of the notarized document and ensure they have access to any necessary follow-up support.

Adopting best practices in remote notarization ensures notaries provide efficient, secure, and professional services. By prioritizing client communication, mastering technology, and adhering to compliance standards, notaries can enhance their reputation and build trust in the growing field of remote notarization.

7   NOTARY FEES & CERTIFICATES

7.1 Fee Structures for Notarial Services

Understanding and implementing appropriate fee structures is crucial for notaries public to ensure their services are fairly compensated while adhering to legal regulations. This chapter explores common fee structures, regulatory considerations, and best practices for transparency and client satisfaction.

Common Fee Structures

1. **Flat Fees:**
   - Many states set statutory limits on the fees notaries can charge for specific acts, such as acknowledgments, oaths, and affirmations.
   - Flat fees provide simplicity and transparency, making them a preferred option for many clients.

2. **Per-Signature Fees:**
   - Notaries may charge fees based on the number of signatures notarized on a document.
   - This structure is common for multi-signature documents, such as loan agreements or contracts.

3. **Hourly Rates:**
   - Some notaries, particularly those providing specialized services like legal or real estate-related notarizations, may charge hourly rates.
   - Hourly fees are typically negotiated in advance and may include preparation time.

4. **Travel Fees:**
   - Mobile notaries can charge additional fees for travel, which may be calculated based on mileage or a flat travel rate.
   - These fees must comply with state-specific regulations, which may limit the maximum amount allowed.

5. **Technology Fees:**
   - For remote notarization, notaries may charge technology fees to cover the cost of secure online platforms.
   - These fees should be clearly itemized and disclosed to clients beforehand.

Regulatory Considerations
1. **State-Imposed Fee Limits:**
   - Most states regulate the maximum fees notaries can charge for various acts. Notaries must stay updated on these limits to avoid non-compliance.
2. **Transparency Requirements:**
   - Many jurisdictions require notaries to provide written fee schedules upon request.
   - Clearly displaying fees on websites or business materials promotes transparency and trust.
3. **Prohibition of Unjustified Fees:**
   - Charging excessive or undisclosed fees is prohibited and may result in penalties, including suspension or revocation of a notary commission.

Best Practices for Fee Management
1. **Clear Communication:**
   - Provide clients with a detailed breakdown of fees, including any additional charges for travel or technology.
   - Obtain client agreement on fees before performing the notarial act.
2. **Itemized Receipts:**
   - Issue receipts that clearly list each service provided and its corresponding fee.
   - Maintain copies of receipts for record-keeping and compliance purposes.
3. **Flexibility and Accessibility:**
   - Consider offering discounts or flexible payment options for underserved or low-income clients.
4. **Regular Updates:**
   - Review and update your fee schedule regularly to reflect changes in state laws or market conditions.

Addressing Disputes Over Fees
1. **Documentation:**
   - Keep detailed records of all transactions, including client communications and agreed-upon fees.
   - Proper documentation can help resolve disputes effectively and protect against claims of overcharging.
2. **Mediation:**
   - Offer to mediate disputes amicably, prioritizing client satisfaction while adhering to legal requirements.
3. **State Authority Guidance:**

o Consult your state's notary authority for guidance on resolving fee-related disputes in compliance with regulations.

Fee structures for notarial services must balance fair compensation with regulatory compliance and client transparency. By adopting clear policies, maintaining detailed records, and prioritizing ethical practices, notaries can build trust and ensure the sustainability of their services.

7.2 Issuing and Managing Certificates of Official Character

Certificates of Official Character serve as a formal recognition of a notary's authority within a jurisdiction. These certificates are essential for establishing trust and verifying a notary's credentials in official matters. This chapter delves into the process of issuing, managing, and utilizing Certificates of Official Character effectively.

What is a Certificate of Official Character?
A Certificate of Official Character is a document issued by a notary's commissioning authority (e.g., the Secretary of State) to confirm the notary's valid commission and authority to perform notarial acts. It is often required for transactions that extend beyond the notary's immediate area of practice.

Purpose of the Certificate
1. **Validation of Authority:**
    o Confirms the legitimacy of the notary's commission for use in legal, financial, and administrative matters.
2. **Cross-Jurisdictional Recognition:**
    o Facilitates the acceptance of notarized documents in different counties, states, or international contexts.
3. **Proof of Compliance:**
    o Demonstrates that the notary complies with applicable laws and regulations.

Process for Issuing a Certificate
1. **Application Submission:**
    o Notaries must apply to the appropriate state or county office to obtain a Certificate of Official Character.
    o The application typically requires the notary's name, commission details, and a nominal processing fee.

2. **Verification of Commission:**
    o The commissioning authority verifies the notary's credentials and standing, ensuring no suspensions or disciplinary actions exist.
3. **Issuance of Certificate:**
    o Once verified, the certificate is issued, usually bearing an official seal or stamp from the commissioning authority.
4. **Delivery Method:**
    o Certificates may be mailed or provided electronically, depending on state procedures.

Managing Certificates of Official Character

1. **Storage and Security:**
    o Keep the certificate in a secure location to prevent unauthorized use.
    o Maintain digital copies for easy access and retrieval when needed.
2. **Renewal and Updates:**
    o Certificates must be renewed in conjunction with the notary's commission renewal.
    o Notify the issuing authority promptly of any changes in personal or professional details, such as address or name changes.
3. **Compliance with Usage Guidelines:**
    o Use the certificate solely for legitimate purposes related to notarial acts.
    o Avoid sharing or lending the certificate to unauthorized parties.

Common Uses of Certificates

1. **Real Estate Transactions:**
    o Often required to validate notarized documents involved in property sales and transfers.
2. **Interstate Transactions:**
    o Used to authenticate notarizations for documents crossing state lines.
3. **Legal Proceedings:**
    o Required in court filings or for verifying affidavits and depositions.

Avoiding Misuse

1. **Unauthorized Replication:**
    o Refrain from making unauthorized copies or modifications to the certificate.

2. **Fraudulent Representation:**
    o Avoid using the certificate to imply authority beyond the scope of a notary's commission.
3. **Reporting Loss or Theft:**
    o Report lost or stolen certificates immediately to the issuing authority to prevent misuse.

Best Practices
1. **Regular Reviews:**
    o Periodically review certificate details to ensure accuracy and validity.
2. **Client Transparency:**
    o Clearly explain the purpose and validity of the certificate when presenting it to clients or authorities.
3. **Adherence to State Laws:**
    o Stay updated on state-specific requirements for managing and renewing Certificates of Official Character.

Conclusion
Certificates of Official Character are vital for establishing a notary's credibility and ensuring the acceptance of their notarial acts across jurisdictions. By following proper issuance and management practices, notaries can maintain the integrity of their role and uphold public trust.

7.3 Handling Name Changes and ID Card Replacements

As public officials, notaries must ensure that their credentials remain accurate and up to date. When a notary undergoes a name change or requires an updated ID card, it is essential to follow proper procedures to maintain compliance and ensure continued service.

Addressing Name Changes
1. **Notifying the Commissioning Authority:**
    o A notary who changes their name due to marriage, divorce, or other legal reasons must promptly notify their state commissioning authority (e.g., Secretary of State).
    o Submit a formal application or name change notification form, often accompanied by legal documentation such as a marriage certificate or court order.
2. **Updating Notarial Records:**
    o Update the notary journal to reflect the name change, ensuring that all entries are consistent and accurate.

- o Notify clients and relevant institutions of the name change to avoid discrepancies in notarized documents.
3. **Obtaining a New Seal or Stamp:**
   - o Acquire a new notarial seal or stamp bearing the updated name, as required by most state regulations.
   - o Retain the old seal or stamp only until the new one is in use, then destroy it to prevent misuse.
4. **Amending Public Records:**
   - o Ensure that the updated name is reflected in public records associated with the notary's commission, such as Certificates of Official Character.

Replacing Notary ID Cards

1. **Reasons for Replacement:**
   - o Lost, stolen, or damaged ID cards.
   - o Name changes or commission renewals that require updated information.
2. **Application Process for Replacement:**
   - o File a replacement request with the commissioning authority, typically involving the completion of a form and payment of a nominal fee.
   - o Provide supporting documentation, such as proof of identity or a copy of the original ID card (if available).
3. **Interim Measures:**
   - o If the notary ID card is lost or stolen, report the incident to the commissioning authority and local law enforcement, if necessary.
   - o Use alternative documentation, such as a Certificate of Official Character, until the replacement is issued.
4. **Receiving and Validating the Replacement:**
   - o Upon receipt of the replacement card, verify that all information is correct.
   - o Notify clients and organizations of the updated credentials to avoid confusion or disruptions in service.

Compliance and Best Practices

1. **Maintaining Accurate Records:**
   - o Keep copies of all communications and documents related to the name change or ID card replacement.
   - o Record the date and details of changes in your notarial journal.

2. **Ensuring Consistency:**
   o Update all related materials, such as business cards, letterhead, and website information, to reflect the changes.
3. **Preventing Fraud:**
   o Securely store notary ID cards and related credentials to prevent unauthorized use.
   o Report any discrepancies or suspicious activities related to your credentials immediately.

Common Challenges and Solutions

1. **Delayed Processing:**
   o Solution: Submit all required documents promptly and confirm receipt with the commissioning authority.
   o Follow up regularly to ensure timely issuance of updated credentials.
2. **Client Confusion:**
   o Solution: Communicate changes to clients clearly, providing assurance that the name change or replacement does not impact the validity of prior notarial acts.
3. **Transition Period Issues:**
   o Solution: Use the current name and credentials until the new ones are issued, and notify all parties of the pending updates.

Handling name changes and ID card replacements efficiently is essential for maintaining the integrity and continuity of notarial services. By following the correct procedures and adhering to state regulations, notaries can ensure that their credentials remain valid and trustworthy.

7.4 Practical Tips for Efficient Fee Management

Efficient fee management is a cornerstone of a successful notarial practice. Proper handling of fees ensures compliance with legal requirements, enhances client satisfaction, and contributes to the sustainability of the notary's business. This chapter provides practical tips to optimize fee management.

Establishing Clear Fee Structures

1. **Understand State Regulations:**
   o Familiarize yourself with state-specific maximum fee limits for notarial acts.
   o Avoid exceeding these limits to remain compliant with regulatory requirements.

2. **Create a Transparent Fee Schedule:**
   - Develop a detailed fee schedule that outlines charges for each notarial service, including additional fees for travel or technology.
   - Make the schedule available on your website, business materials, or upon request.
3. **Incorporate Optional Fees:**
   - Identify services that may warrant additional fees, such as document preparation or rush services, and ensure they are lawful and clearly communicated.

Streamlining Fee Collection

1. **Offer Multiple Payment Options:**
   - Accept various payment methods, such as cash, checks, credit cards, and digital wallets, to accommodate client preferences.
   - Use secure payment systems to protect client information.
2. **Collect Fees Upfront:**
   - Request payment before performing the notarial act to avoid disputes or unpaid fees.
   - Clearly explain the payment process during initial client interactions.
3. **Use Invoicing Systems:**
   - Utilize invoicing software to issue professional, itemized invoices that detail services provided and associated fees.
   - Include due dates and payment instructions to ensure timely payments.

Maintaining Accurate Records

1. **Log Transactions:**
   - Record all fee-related transactions in your notarial journal, including the date, service provided, and amount received.
   - This practice ensures accountability and simplifies financial tracking.
2. **Keep Receipts:**
   - Provide clients with receipts for all payments and retain copies for your records.
   - Use electronic receipts for a streamlined and eco-friendly approach.
3. **Track Expenses:**
   - Monitor and document business-related expenses, such as supplies, travel, and software subscriptions, to manage costs effectively.

Enhancing Client Transparency
1. **Communicate Fees Clearly:**
   - Discuss fees with clients upfront to avoid surprises or disputes.
   - Provide written confirmation of agreed-upon charges when necessary.
2. **Explain Additional Charges:**
   - Clearly outline circumstances that may result in additional fees, such as after-hours services or extended travel distances.
3. **Be Consistent:**
   - Apply your fee structure uniformly to all clients to maintain fairness and trust.

Managing Disputes
1. **Maintain Documentation:**
   - Keep detailed records of all client communications and agreements related to fees.
   - Use these records to address any disputes professionally and effectively.
2. **Offer Resolutions:**
   - If a client disputes a fee, listen to their concerns and offer a reasonable resolution, such as clarifying the charges or adjusting the fee if warranted.
3. **Escalate When Necessary:**
   - If a dispute cannot be resolved amicably, consult your state's notary authority or seek legal advice to protect your interests.

Leveraging Technology for Efficiency
1. **Use Fee Management Software:**
   - Adopt software that automates invoicing, payment tracking, and reporting.
   - This reduces administrative burdens and minimizes errors.
2. **Track Trends:**
   - Analyze fee patterns over time to identify high-demand services or opportunities to optimize your pricing strategy.
3. **Stay Updated:**
   - Regularly review updates to fee regulations or technological tools that enhance fee management capabilities.

Building Client Trust
1. **Be Transparent:**
    o   Transparency in fee structures and transactions fosters trust and encourages repeat business.
2. **Show Professionalism:**
    o   Demonstrate professionalism in all financial dealings, ensuring clients feel confident in the value of your services.
3. **Provide Value:**
    o   Beyond competitive pricing, focus on delivering high-quality service to justify your fees and build a strong reputation.

Efficient fee management is essential for both compliance and client satisfaction. By adopting transparent practices, leveraging technology, and maintaining accurate records, notaries can manage their fees effectively while enhancing their professional reputation.

8   LEGAL CONTEXT & FRAMEWORK

8.1 Public Officers Law

Public Officers Law establishes the framework for the appointment, responsibilities, and ethical conduct of public officers, including notaries public. Understanding these provisions is critical for notaries to fulfill their roles effectively and maintain public trust.

Key Provisions of Public Officers Law for Notaries
1. **Appointment and Qualification:**
    o   The law outlines eligibility criteria for notaries, such as age, citizenship, and residency requirements.
    o   It specifies the process for applying, renewing, and resigning from a notary commission.
2. **Oath of Office:**
    o   Public Officers Law requires notaries to take an oath of office upon appointment.
    o   This oath signifies the notary's commitment to ethical conduct and the faithful execution of duties.

3. **Ethical Standards:**
   - Notaries must uphold integrity and impartiality in their official acts, avoiding conflicts of interest and misuse of authority.
   - The law prohibits public officers from using their position for personal gain.

Responsibilities Under Public Officers Law

1. **Record-Keeping:**
   - Notaries are required to maintain accurate records of their official acts, including detailed logs of notarizations.
   - Public Officers Law often mandates the retention of these records for a specified period.

2. **Accessibility of Services:**
   - Notaries must ensure their services are reasonably available to the public without discrimination.

3. **Compliance with State Regulations:**
   - Adhering to the rules governing notarial acts, including document verification and identity authentication, is essential under Public Officers Law.

Penalties for Violations

1. **Administrative Sanctions:**
   - Non-compliance may result in suspension, fines, or revocation of the notary's commission.

2. **Civil and Criminal Liability:**
   - Misconduct, such as fraudulent certifications or discrimination, can expose notaries to lawsuits or criminal charges.

3. **Ethical Repercussions:**
   - Violations of Public Officers Law can damage a notary's reputation and undermine public confidence in their role.

Best Practices for Adhering to Public Officers Law

1. **Education and Awareness:**
   - Stay informed about updates to Public Officers Law and related regulations.
   - Attend training sessions and workshops to enhance knowledge of legal and ethical obligations.

2. **Transparent Operations:** Clearly communicate fees, procedures, and limitations of notarial services to clients.

3. **Secure Handling of Tools and Records:** Ensure the proper safeguarding of notarial seals, journals, and other official materials to prevent misuse.

Importance of Public Officers Law in Notarial Practices
1. **Defining Authority:**
    - Public Officers Law clarifies the scope of authority granted to notaries, preventing overreach and misuse of power.
2. **Ensuring Accountability:**
    - By establishing clear responsibilities and penalties, the law holds notaries accountable for their actions.
3. **Promoting Public Trust:**
    - Adherence to the law reinforces the reliability and integrity of notarial acts, ensuring public confidence in notaries' roles.

Public Officers Law serves as a cornerstone for the ethical and effective performance of notarial duties. By understanding and complying with its provisions, notaries can uphold their commitment to public service while mitigating risks of legal or ethical violations.

8.2 Real Property Law

Real property law governs transactions involving land and real estate, where notarial acts play a crucial role in ensuring the validity and enforceability of documents. This chapter explores the intersection of notarial practices and real property law, highlighting key responsibilities and best practices for notaries.

Key Roles of Notaries in Real Property Transactions
1. **Acknowledgments:**
    - Notaries verify the identity of parties executing real estate documents and confirm their willingness to sign.
    - Acknowledgments are essential for deeds, mortgages, and other real property instruments to be recorded.
2. **Administering Oaths and Affirmations:**
    - Notaries may administer oaths or affirmations for affidavits required in real property transactions.
    - These sworn statements ensure that factual claims in property dealings are accurate and legally binding.
3. **Document Authentication:**
    - Authenticating documents for real property transactions adds credibility and ensures they meet statutory requirements for recording.

Common Documents Requiring Notarization in Real Property Law

1. **Deeds:**
   - Warranty deeds, quitclaim deeds, and grant deeds require notarization to transfer property ownership legally.
2. **Mortgages and Deeds of Trust:**
   - Notarization ensures these documents are enforceable and protect lenders' interests.
3. **Easements and Leases:**
   - Long-term leases and easement agreements often require notarization for recording purposes.
4. **Powers of Attorney:**
   - Powers of attorney used in real estate transactions must be notarized to be valid.

Compliance with Real Property Law

1. **Identity Verification:**
   - Verify the identity of all signers using government-issued identification to prevent fraud.
2. **Understanding State-Specific Requirements:**
   - Familiarize yourself with state-specific provisions regarding notarization of real property documents.
3. **Proper Use of Notarial Seals:**
   - Ensure the notarial seal is affixed correctly and includes all required information for real property filings.
4. **Record-Keeping:**
   - Maintain accurate logs of notarizations related to real property transactions as part of compliance obligations.

Challenges in Real Property Transactions

1. **Complex Legal Requirements:**
   - Real property laws vary significantly across jurisdictions, making it essential for notaries to stay informed.
2. **Fraud Prevention:**
   - Real estate transactions are often targeted by fraudsters, requiring notaries to exercise heightened vigilance.
3. **Coordination with Multiple Parties:**
   - Notaries must coordinate effectively with buyers, sellers, lenders, and attorneys to ensure seamless transactions.

Best Practices for Notaries in Real Property Transactions

1. **Continuing Education:**
   - Stay updated on changes in real property law and attend training sessions specific to real estate notarization.

2. **Meticulous Attention to Detail:**
   - o Double-check all documents for completeness and accuracy before notarization.
3. **Effective Communication:**
   - o Communicate clearly with all parties to explain the notarization process and address any concerns.
4. **Using Secure Platforms:**
   - o For remote notarizations, use state-approved platforms to ensure compliance with legal standards.

Importance of Real Property Law in Notarial Practices
1. **Ensuring Legal Validity:**
   - o Notarized real property documents must comply with the law to be enforceable and recordable.
2. **Facilitating Trust:**
   - o Notaries provide assurance to all parties that transactions are conducted ethically and transparently.
3. **Preventing Disputes:**
   - o Proper notarization reduces the likelihood of legal challenges to real property documents.

Real property law underscores the critical role of notaries in facilitating secure and legally compliant real estate transactions. By adhering to best practices and understanding their responsibilities under this legal framework, notaries can contribute to the integrity and efficiency of property dealings.

8.3 Judiciary Law

Judiciary law plays a significant role in shaping the framework within which notaries operate. By addressing legal procedures, ethical standards, and the resolution of disputes, judiciary law ensures that notarial acts align with the broader principles of justice and fairness.

Key Provisions of Judiciary Law for Notaries
1. **Court-Related Notarial Acts:**
   - o Judiciary law often governs notarial acts performed in conjunction with legal proceedings, such as affidavits, depositions, and sworn statements.
   - o Notaries must ensure that such acts meet court standards for admissibility and accuracy.

2. **Authentication of Documents:**
    o Judiciary law provides guidelines on the authentication of notarized documents for use in judicial and administrative proceedings.
    o Notaries may be required to certify that documents comply with jurisdiction-specific requirements.
3. **Impartiality and Neutrality:**
    o Judiciary law emphasizes the importance of impartiality in notarial acts, particularly when they are related to legal disputes.
    o Notaries must avoid conflicts of interest and maintain neutrality in all professional interactions.

Responsibilities Under Judiciary Law
1. **Diligence in Verification:**
    o Judiciary law mandates thorough verification of signer identity and intent, ensuring that notarized documents are genuine and executed willingly.
2. **Proper Record Maintenance:**
    o Maintaining comprehensive records of notarial acts is critical for accountability, particularly when such records may be used as evidence in legal proceedings.
3. **Adherence to Procedural Requirements:**
    o Notaries must follow precise procedural steps, such as administering oaths or affirmations, as outlined in judiciary law.

Penalties for Non-Compliance
1. **Judicial Sanctions:**
    o Failure to comply with judiciary law can result in judicial sanctions, including fines or contempt of court charges.
2. **Revocation of Notary Commission:**
    o Non-compliance may lead to disciplinary actions, including suspension or revocation of a notary's commission.
3. **Civil and Criminal Liability:**
    o Negligence or fraudulent actions can expose notaries to lawsuits or criminal prosecution.

Best Practices for Compliance with Judiciary Law
1. **Education and Training:**
    o Participate in training programs that emphasize judiciary law and its implications for notarial practice.

2. **Collaboration with Legal Professionals:**
   - Work closely with attorneys and court officials to ensure compliance with judiciary law in court-related notarial acts.
3. **Ongoing Self-Audit:**
   - Regularly review your notarial practices to ensure they align with judiciary law and other applicable regulations.

Role of Judiciary Law in Upholding Public Confidence
1. **Ensuring Legal Validity:**
   - Judiciary law ensures that notarized documents meet the standards required for legal and judicial purposes.
2. **Protecting Signers' Rights:**
   - By mandating impartiality and thorough verification, judiciary law safeguards the rights and interests of all parties involved.
3. **Reinforcing Ethical Standards:**
   - Judiciary law serves as a foundation for ethical conduct, promoting trust and reliability in notarial acts.

Judiciary law is integral to notarial practice, ensuring that acts performed by notaries contribute to the administration of justice. By adhering to its provisions, notaries uphold their responsibility to the legal system and the public, ensuring fairness, accuracy, and trustworthiness in all their professional endeavors.

8.4 Penal Law

Understanding and adhering to penal laws is a critical aspect of notarial practice. Notaries must be well-versed in legal provisions to avoid actions that may result in criminal liability, ensuring their duties are performed ethically and within the boundaries of the law.

Overview of Relevant Penal Laws
1. **Forgery and Fraud Prevention:**
   - Penal laws strictly prohibit falsifying signatures, seals, or documents.
   - Notaries must verify the authenticity of documents and signatures to prevent fraudulent activities.
2. **False Certification:**
   - Certifying a document or signature without proper verification is considered a criminal offense.
   - Notaries must always follow due diligence procedures to confirm the validity of certifications.

3. **Misuse of Notarial Seal:**
   - The unauthorized use of a notary's seal for personal or third-party gain is a violation of penal law.
   - Secure storage and use of the notarial seal are essential to avoid misuse.

Responsibilities to Avoid Criminal Liability

1. **Impartiality:**
   - Acting impartially and avoiding conflicts of interest protects notaries from legal challenges.
   - Refuse services where impartiality cannot be maintained.
2. **Proper Record-Keeping:**
   - Maintain detailed records of all notarial acts, as incomplete or inaccurate logs can lead to legal scrutiny.
   - Ensure compliance with state-specific record retention requirements.
3. **Adherence to Identity Verification Standards:**
   - Follow legal standards for verifying signer identities, including the use of approved identification documents and methods.
   - Avoid notarizing documents for individuals whose identity cannot be conclusively verified.

Consequences of Non-Compliance

1. **Criminal Penalties:**
   - Violations of penal laws can result in fines, imprisonment, or both.
   - Examples include knowingly notarizing forged documents or engaging in fraudulent activities.
2. **Revocation of Notary Commission:**
   - Criminal acts can lead to the suspension or permanent revocation of a notary's commission.
3. **Civil Liability:**
   - Clients or third parties harmed by a notary's unlawful actions may file lawsuits for damages.

Best Practices to Stay Compliant

1. **Continuing Education:**
   - Participate in training programs to stay updated on changes in penal laws and best practices.
   - Familiarize yourself with specific penal codes relevant to notarial work in your jurisdiction.

2. **Use Secure Platforms:**
   - When performing remote notarizations, use state-approved platforms that ensure compliance with identity verification and record-keeping laws.
3. **Seek Legal Counsel:**
   - Consult with legal professionals when unsure about the legality of a notarial act or process.

Role of Notaries in Upholding Legal Integrity

1. **Acting as Gatekeepers:**
   - Notaries play a crucial role in deterring fraud and ensuring the legitimacy of transactions.
2. **Educating Clients:**
   - Inform clients about the importance of notarization and the legal standards involved.
3. **Promoting Ethical Standards:**
   - Lead by example by adhering to the highest ethical and legal standards in every notarization.

Penal laws serve as a vital framework for ensuring the integrity of notarial practices. By adhering to these laws and implementing best practices, notaries can avoid criminal liability, protect their professional reputation, and contribute to a trustworthy legal system.

8.5 Executive Law

Executive law governs the duties, responsibilities, and limitations of notaries public. Understanding the executive law relevant to their jurisdiction is essential for notaries to perform their duties within the scope of their authority and maintain compliance with legal standards.

Key Provisions of Executive Law for Notaries

1. **Appointment and Commissioning:**
   - Executive law outlines the process for appointing and commissioning notaries.
   - Notaries must meet eligibility requirements, such as age, residency, and background checks, as specified by their state.
2. **Defined Scope of Authority:**
   - The law specifies the acts that notaries are authorized to perform, including acknowledgments, oaths, affirmations, and witness signatures.

- o Performing acts outside the defined scope can result in penalties or revocation of commission.

3. **Responsibilities and Duties:**
   - o Notaries are required to ensure that signers are competent and willing to execute documents.
   - o Executive law mandates the use of a notarial seal or stamp and proper record-keeping for all notarial acts.

4. **Prohibited Acts:**
   - o Notaries must not offer legal advice unless they are licensed attorneys.
   - o They are prohibited from notarizing documents in which they have a personal or financial interest.

Compliance with Executive Law

1. **Renewal of Commission:**
   - o Notaries must adhere to renewal procedures, including completing applications and paying fees, as specified by executive law.

2. **Record Retention:**
   - o Maintaining accurate records, such as journals of notarial acts, is often required.
   - o Executive law may specify the retention period for these records.

3. **Use of Approved Tools:**
   - o Notarial seals, stamps, and electronic platforms must comply with standards established under executive law.

4. **Identity Verification Standards:**
   - o The law often specifies acceptable forms of identification, such as government-issued IDs, to verify the identity of signers.

Penalties for Non-Compliance

1. **Administrative Actions:**
   - o Violations of executive law can result in fines, suspension, or revocation of the notary's commission.

2. **Civil Liability:**
   - o Notaries may face lawsuits from clients or third parties harmed by negligent or unauthorized acts.

3. **Criminal Charges:**
   - o Intentional violations, such as falsifying records or engaging in fraud, may lead to criminal prosecution.

Best Practices for Adhering to Executive Law
1. **Education and Training:**
   - Stay informed about updates to executive law and complete any mandatory training programs.
2. **Thorough Documentation:**
   - Maintain detailed and accurate records of all notarial acts, ensuring compliance with legal standards.
3. **Seeking Clarification:**
   - Consult with legal professionals or state authorities when unclear about the application of executive law.

Importance of Executive Law in Notarial Practices
1. **Establishing Accountability:**
   - Executive law provides a framework for holding notaries accountable for their actions.
2. **Protecting Public Trust:**
   - By adhering to the law, notaries reinforce the integrity and trustworthiness of their role.
3. **Guiding Ethical Conduct:**
   - Executive law serves as a guideline for ethical decision-making in complex scenarios.

9   TOOLS & TECHNIQUES

9.1 Multiple Choice Test Taking Strategies

Mastering multiple-choice test-taking strategies is essential for notaries preparing for certification exams. Effective strategies can help candidates approach questions with confidence, manage time efficiently, and maximize their scores. This chapter provides practical tips for excelling in multiple-choice exams.

Preparing for the Test
1. **Understand the Test Format:**
   - Familiarize yourself with the number of questions, time limits, and subject areas covered.
   - Review sample questions or practice exams to understand the types of questions commonly asked.

2. **Review Key Concepts:**
   - Focus on understanding notarial laws, procedures, and ethical standards that are likely to appear on the exam.
   - Create study aids, such as flashcards or summary notes, to reinforce essential knowledge.
3. **Practice Regularly:**
   - Take timed practice tests to simulate exam conditions and build confidence.
   - Review answers thoroughly to identify strengths and areas needing improvement.

Strategies During the Exam
1. **Read Questions Carefully:**
   - Pay close attention to the wording of each question, especially qualifiers like "always," "never," or "except."
   - Identify the key idea or concept being tested.
2. **Eliminate Incorrect Answers:**
   - Narrow down choices by eliminating answers that are clearly incorrect.
   - Focus on the remaining options to improve the odds of selecting the correct answer.
3. **Look for Clues in the Question:**
   - Use context clues in the question to guide your choice.
   - Watch for keywords that align with specific notarial concepts or procedures.
4. **Answer Easy Questions First:**
   - Begin with questions you are confident about to build momentum and save time for more challenging ones.
   - Mark difficult questions and return to them later if time allows.
5. **Use Logical Reasoning:**
   - For questions where the answer is unclear, use logical reasoning to make an educated guess.
   - Eliminate unlikely answers to focus on the most probable choice.
6. **Watch for Trick Questions:**
   - Be cautious of questions that seem straightforward but include subtle traps, such as double negatives or unusual phrasing.

Time Management

1. **Allocate Time Wisely:**
   - Divide the total test time by the number of questions to determine how much time to spend on each.
   - Keep track of time and ensure you move through the test at a steady pace.
2. **Don't Dwell on One Question:**
   - Avoid spending too much time on a single question. Mark it and return to it if time permits.
3. **Leave No Question Unanswered:**
   - If there is no penalty for incorrect answers, ensure every question is answered, even if it requires an educated guess.

Reviewing Your Answers

1. **Double-Check Your Work:**
   - If time permits, review your answers to ensure they are accurate and complete.
   - Look for skipped questions or mismarked answers.
2. **Trust Your Instincts:**
   - Avoid changing an answer unless you are certain of a mistake. Your first choice is often correct.
3. **Revisit Marked Questions:**
   - Return to questions you marked as challenging and review them with a fresh perspective.

Test Day Tips

1. **Stay Calm and Focused:**
   - Take deep breaths to manage test anxiety and maintain concentration.
   - Approach each question with a clear mind and confidence in your preparation.
2. **Read Instructions Carefully:**
   - Before beginning the test, review the instructions to ensure you understand the format and rules.
3. **Bring Necessary Materials:**
   - Ensure you have required items, such as identification, pencils, erasers, or calculators, as specified by the test administrator.

Success in multiple-choice exams requires a combination of preparation, strategic thinking, and time management. By implementing these strategies, notary candidates can navigate their exams effectively, boosting their confidence and performance.

9.2 Common Mistakes and How to Avoid Them

When taking multiple-choice exams, common mistakes can undermine a candidate's performance, even with thorough preparation. Recognizing these pitfalls and learning strategies to avoid them can make a significant difference in achieving a high score.

Misreading the Question
1. **The Mistake:**
   - Skimming over questions too quickly can lead to misunderstanding key details or missing critical words, such as "not" or "except."
   - Misinterpreting what the question is asking often results in selecting an incorrect answer.
2. **How to Avoid It:**
   - Read each question carefully, paying attention to qualifiers and important terms.
   - Highlight or underline key phrases if permitted.

Focusing Too Much on Difficult Questions
1. **The Mistake:**
   - Spending excessive time on challenging questions can cause you to rush through the rest of the test.
   - This may lead to unanswered questions or errors on easier items.
2. **How to Avoid It:**
   - Move past difficult questions and return to them later if time permits.
   - Use a system to mark questions you want to revisit, such as circling or flagging them.

Ignoring Instructions
1. **The Mistake:**
   - Failing to read or follow the test instructions can lead to errors, such as selecting multiple answers when only one is required.
   - Misunderstanding the format may also lead to avoidable mistakes.
2. **How to Avoid It:**
   - Carefully review all instructions before beginning the test.
   - Clarify any uncertainties with the test proctor if allowed.

Overanalyzing Questions

1. **The Mistake:**
   - Overthinking can lead to second-guessing initial answers and creating confusion.
   - Candidates may interpret a question too deeply, looking for complexity that isn't there.
2. **How to Avoid It:**
   - Trust your preparation and instincts.
   - Stick to the facts and concepts you studied without overcomplicating the question.

Not Managing Time Effectively

1. **The Mistake:**
   - Poor time management can result in leaving questions unanswered or rushing through the final section of the test.
2. **How to Avoid It:**
   - Allocate a specific amount of time for each question or section based on the total test duration.
   - Regularly check the time and adjust your pace as needed.

Leaving Questions Blank

1. **The Mistake:**
   - Skipping questions without returning to answer them leaves potential points unearned.
   - This is especially problematic when there is no penalty for incorrect answers.
2. **How to Avoid It:**
   - Always provide an answer, even if you need to make an educated guess.
   - Use elimination strategies to improve the likelihood of selecting the correct option.

Failing to Review Answers

1. **The Mistake:**
   - Not reviewing answers before submitting the test can result in missed opportunities to correct errors or complete skipped questions.
2. **How to Avoid It:**
   - Reserve time at the end of the test to review all answers.
   - Double-check skipped or marked questions to ensure they are addressed.

Misusing Study Time
1. **The Mistake:**
   - Focusing on areas of strength while neglecting weaker subjects may result in unbalanced preparation.
   - Relying solely on memorization without understanding concepts can also backfire.
2. **How to Avoid It:**
   - Use study time strategically, giving extra attention to challenging topics.
   - Prioritize understanding the material over rote memorization.

Letting Anxiety Take Over
1. **The Mistake:**
   - Test anxiety can cause a lack of focus, misreading questions, or rushing through the exam.
2. **How to Avoid It:**
   - Practice relaxation techniques, such as deep breathing, before and during the test.
   - Prepare thoroughly to build confidence and reduce anxiety.

Overlooking Details in Answer Choices
1. **The Mistake:**
   - Choosing the first answer that appears correct without fully reading the other options can lead to missed nuances.
2. **How to Avoid It:**
   - Review all answer choices before making a selection.
   - Compare options carefully to identify the best answer.

Avoiding common test-taking mistakes is as important as mastering the content of the exam. By adopting these strategies, candidates can approach their tests with greater confidence, reduce errors, and optimize their performance.

9.3 Effective Study Techniques

Effective study techniques are essential for mastering the material required for notary certification exams. By adopting structured approaches and leveraging proven methods, candidates can enhance their retention, comprehension, and confidence. This chapter outlines practical strategies to maximize your study sessions.

Set Clear Goals

Before diving into your studies, define specific objectives for each session. Break the material into manageable sections, such as legal terminology, procedures, or state-specific regulations. Prioritize areas where you feel less confident and allocate additional time to those topics. Having clear goals keeps you focused and ensures steady progress.

Create a Study Schedule

Consistency is key to effective studying. Develop a schedule that dedicates specific times to studying each day or week. Break sessions into manageable chunks, such as 25- to 50-minute intervals, followed by short breaks. This approach, often called the Pomodoro Technique, helps maintain focus and reduces burnout.

Use Active Learning Techniques

Active engagement with the material improves retention compared to passive reading. Techniques such as summarizing sections in your own words, teaching the material to others, or creating visual aids like charts and diagrams make the information more memorable. Practice answering potential exam questions to simulate real test conditions.

Leverage Flashcards

Flashcards are an excellent tool for reinforcing key concepts, definitions, and procedures. Write a question or term on one side and its explanation or answer on the other. Use physical cards or digital tools like Quizlet to quiz yourself regularly, focusing on cards you find challenging.

Take Practice Tests

Simulating the exam environment with practice tests helps identify areas of strength and those needing improvement. Review your answers to understand mistakes and refine your study focus. Practice tests also build familiarity with the exam format, reducing test-day anxiety.

Join a Study Group

Collaborating with peers allows you to exchange knowledge, clarify doubts, and gain new perspectives. Study groups can also hold you accountable and keep you motivated. Ensure the group remains focused and productive by setting agendas for each meeting.

Utilize Multiple Resources

Supplement your primary study materials with additional resources such as online tutorials, video lectures, and professional notary guides. Diversifying your sources enhances understanding and provides alternative explanations for complex topics.

Stay Organized

Keep your study materials, notes, and resources well-organized. Use binders, digital folders, or apps to categorize information by topics, making it easier to review specific sections. Highlight key points and create summaries for quick reference.

Incorporate Spaced Repetition

Review material periodically instead of cramming it all at once. Spaced repetition strengthens memory by revisiting information over increasing intervals. Tools like Anki can help automate this process and optimize your review schedule.

Take Care of Your Health

Physical and mental well-being directly impact your ability to study effectively. Ensure you get adequate sleep, maintain a balanced diet, and incorporate regular exercise into your routine. Manage stress with relaxation techniques like mindfulness or meditation.

10 COMMISSIONED NOTARY PUBLIC IN NEW YORK STATE

10.1 Introduction

If you have purchased this book, this means you have every intention to take the examination that you may be qualified to be a Notary Public within the state of New York. There is the chance that you would want to know what are the requirements needed for you or for another person to be a notary public in New York? The concept of notaries public, as they are wont to be called in the plural, is defined by the New York State Department of State, as those individuals who have been commissioned by the Secretary of State.

First, there must be a distinction drawn with regards to notaries public. There might be some confusion that arises as to whether attorneys-at-law can be notaries public, or is the notary public considered to be an attorney? The New York Department of State outlines first the functions of a notary public wherein they are permitted to perform certain functions. These include:

- The administration of oaths and affirmations
- The taking down of affidavits and depositions
- The receipt and certification of acknowledgements and proof of written instruments such as deeds of sale or land transfer, mortgages and the powers of attorney.
- The issuance of demands, but in accordance with the provisions of Notary Public Law, these demands are only issued for the acceptance and payment of foreign and inland bills of exchange, the issuance of promissory notes and obligations in writing which are considered part of negotiable instruments. It must be noted that in this latter circumstance, the notaries public are permitted to protest the non-payment of these demands when presented, and these are done free of charge.

Due to the nature of their functions, employments for notaries public are centered on institutions that encounter a high volume of paperwork that requires the presence of a person who is able to address these depositions, deeds, various written legal instruments and other similar documentations that are involved in the operations of these institutions. As such, banks, law firms that encounter a high volume of financial and real estate transactions are most likely to require the need for a notary public in their offices. As a prospective notary public, it is expected that you are to familiarize yourself with these functions.

Back to the question posed in the previous paragraph. Not all notaries public are attorneys-at-law by profession, and likewise, not all attorneys-at-law are notaries public. However, there are special dispensations for attorneys-at-law, as they are allowed to be notaries public without the need for further examination. It is important to note that the commission of a notary public only lasts for four years.

10.2 Obtaining a Notary Commission in NY

The Notary Public, as defined by the Department of State of New York, is an individual who has been commissioned for four years by the Secretary of State of their respective state, which in this context is New York State. For those who are interested on how to obtain the commission, the following procedures are to be done: to commence the process of qualification for this position, the interested individual must submit their original application and the fee to the Division of Licensing Services. As of this writing, the fee for the application process costs $60 dollars, the fee may have undergone changes. It would be a good idea to inquire about the current fee for the Notary Public application at the office of the Secretary of State.

10.3 Application for Notary Public?

The application for a notary public includes the oath of office, an important and essential aspect for the qualification process of the applicant, which must be sworn to and notarized. Aside from the submission of the form and the payment of the corresponding fee, the applicant must also submit their pass slip. This pass slip is important in the application process as this signifies that the applicant has passed the examination needed to qualify as a notary public.

Examinations to be a notary public are scheduled all over New York State. There are exceptions to the examinations for Notary Public, as Attorneys who are permitted to practice in New York State may be granted their commission by the Secretary of State without the need to pass the notary public examination. It is important to reiterate that once commissioned by the Secretary of State, the individual serves as a notary public for only four years. Other individuals who are exempt from the Notary Public Examination are Court Clerks of the Unified Court System.

10.4 Jurisdiction of Notarial Acts

The concept of jurisdiction is not one to be taken for granted as the concept of jurisdiction defines where a commissioned notary public is permitted to practice, as well as take cognizance of the instruments that they have notarized. Earlier, it was stated that the Secretary of State of New York carries the sole responsibilities for the commission of notaries public for New York. This does not entail however that the commissioned individual is permitted to operate in any county in New York. The jurisdictional area of the commissioned notary public extends only towards their county of residence. Once the Secretary of State receives the application for the notary public and subsequently approves it, the commission is forwarded along with the original oath of office, and the signature of the notary public to the county clerk. Jurisdiction and venue as terms may refer to the same concept, however, jurisdiction in this manner, refers more on the area wherein the notary public may operate in New York State, while venue refers to the place wherein the notary public had performed the notarial act and must be indicated in the jurat of the notarized instrument or document that forms the basis of the notarial act. The inclusion of the venue cannot be omitted from the notarial act.

10.5 County Clerk's Role with Commission?

Once the County Clerk receives the commission that was issued by the Office of the Secretary of State, the county clerk records the commission and the signature. At this point, should the pubic wish to ascertain the identity and verify that a certain individual is qualified to be a notary public, they may access the records maintained by the county clerk to ascertain that the official signature of the individual corresponds with the documents that are notarized by the individual who purports to be a duly commissioned Notary Public in the state and in the county where they have the jurisdiction. Upon the request of the individual who wishes to verify the authority of the notary public, the county clerk will be able to issue an attestation that the notary does has the authority to sign. It is expected that this occurrence will take place when the documents to be notarized are to be used outside the jurisdiction of New York State.

10.6 Out-of-State Use of Notarized Documents

The notary who regularly encounters documents from other counties aside from their county of residence has the option for an action of filing for a certificate of official character with the offices of the County Clerks of New York State.

10.7 Residency Requirements for a NY Notary

As a general rule, it is expected that to be a notary public in New York State, you are a resident of the county wherein you are expected to apply for your commission. There are circumstances however wherein a non-resident of New York State may apply for a notarial commission though they do not reside within New York State itself. They are referred to as non-resident residents.

Nonresident residents are applicants for notary commissions who come from other states. These include attorneys from other states licensed by their respective bars to practice in New York State. Such attorneys maintain offices within New York State; they are considered citizens of the county where their place of business is located. Nonresident non-lawyers who also have offices or companies in New York may be notaries public. For an outsider to become a notary public, their oath of office and signature must be submitted to the county clerk's office where their office or place of business is situated.

11   THE RESPONSABILITIES

This chapter outlines the responsibilities of what a notary public is expected to do while in the performance of their tasks. The distinction between what a notary public and attorney at law is outlined in the responsibilities that a notary public is allowed to perform while commissioned by the Secretary of State. At this point, you may have questions as to what a notary public does. In the previous chapter, we have outlined the four-fold responsibilities of a notary public and in this chapter we are able to elaborate more on the overall responsibilities.

As with many professional organizations however, there are expected rules of professional conduct that a person who has been commissioned as a notary public is expected to abide by. While a notary public does get involved in the legal aspects of written instruments and even negotiable instruments, there are certain tasks that they are permitted to perform within the purview of the scope of function of the notary public. These tasks that the notary public are empowered to perform are limited in that they are only permitted to handle instruments that pertain to sales, and the transfer of real property. Even these are limited to specific extent that will be elaborated later on in this book. Of note, another section of this book is dedicated towards the adaptation of the newer practice of remote notarization in light of the effects of the pandemic. The entire process and prerequisites for the use of remote notarization will be elaborated on in this chapter to ensure that you are able to remotely notarize instruments within the scope permitted by the New York State Department of State.

What are the liabilities of a Notary Public?

The Secretary of State and the Department of State of New York state that the use of the office of the notary public for purposes other than what has been specifically provided for in the Notary Public Law of New York is a serious offense. Later in this book you will encounter the various offenses that the Notary Public can be held liable for. These include the illegal practice of law by a non-attorney, which will be elaborated later on in this chapter as a series of offenses. Forgeries which can result in felonies on the part of the notary public who engages in the act; and even the inability to ascertain the identity. It must be recalled that the responsibilities of the Notary Public are a public office and that the notarial act which is committed may result in the Notary Public being held liable for whatever errors may result from the notarial act, to not only the State, but also to their constituent who requested the notarial act.

A good idea throughout the use of this book is to read through the provisions on Notary Public Law and remember the acts that are permitted of the Notary Public to ensure that you do not perform the acts that would lead to felonies and misdemeanors on your part as a Notary Public.

Are Notaries Public permitted to take acknowledgments and affidavits over the phone without the affiant making an appearance?

No. This practice is prohibited by the provisions of professional conduct under New York State Law. An acknowledgement or affidavit cannot be taken over the phone or by any other means of communication unless the individual making the acknowledgment or affidavit appears in person before the officiating notary.

The Notary Public Law of New York State draws attention to the judicial declarations that involve these instances:

In the case *Matter of Napolis,* it is stated that the courts condemn the practice of notaries who execute acknowledgments or affidavits without the presence of a party that requested for the acknowledgment. It is noted that the courts will penalize the severity of the professional misconduct that was performed by the notary public through the erroneous notarial act as this is a violation of their notarial duty. (169 App. Div. 469, 472).

The Notary Public Law of New York State cites the case of *Matter of Gottheim* (153 App. Div., 779, 782), where it is stated that, on the good faith of the acknowledgments that are executed by the notary public are the titles of real property, and the only form of security that the parties concerned may have is the faith with which the commissioned notary public or the commissioner of deeds may have when they request the personal appearance of the concerned parties when these instruments or documents are presented to the notary public, and that this faith in their duty entitles them to refuse the execution of the notarial act with the exception that the parties concerned are personally known to the notary public, or if the notary public or commissioner of deeds was able to satisfactorily ascertain the identities of the parties who execute the instruments without the shadow of a doubt.

What does the Administration of Oaths entail?

The simplest and easiest manner by which an oath may be **lawfully** administered is found in the case of *Bookman vs. City of New York* (200 N.Y. 53, 56) where the notary public asks if the affiant solemnly swears that the contents of the affidavit that was subscribed to the notary public is correct in its contents and valid in their provisions.

It is important at this point to ascertain that the substance within the instrument is exactly what the affiant swears it to be, and that it is valid on its face. In the event that the notary public encounters individuals who conscientiously decline to take an oath, the following affirmation may be utilized in its place. This affirmation used is just as legally binding as the oath administered in the previous instance. In this instance, what is asked by the Notary Public of the affiant in question is that to their knowledge, does the affiant solemnly and sincerely declare that the statements made under the oath are correct and true.

The cases of *People ex rel. Kenyon vs., Sutherland,* 81 N.Y.1, and *O'Reilly vs. People,* 86 N.Y., 154,158,161 cite the following conditions for the administration of oaths by a notary public:

Whatever the form adopted, it (the oath or affirmation) must be taken in the presence of an officer who has the authority to duly administer the said oath. Two important requisites for the completion of a notarial act are that the act must be unequivocal and present, the affiant consciously takes upon himself the obligation of an oath when they swear to the oath administered to them.

The administration of the oath is an important consideration under the laws of the New York Notary Public Law, and the Secretary of State frowns when the administration of oaths is improperly performed.

May a Notary Public engage in the Practice of Law?

Unless the Notary Public happens to be a lawyer, the Notary Public is prohibited from direct or indirect engagement in the practice of law. The unauthorized practice of law by the Notary Public will subject them to their removal from office by the Secretary of State, with possible imprisonment, fines or both.

What are the acts that a Notary Public is not allowed to engage in?

There are four acts that a Notary Public is not allowed to perform, as these constitute an unauthorized practice of law outside the scope of the functions of a Notary Public.

These are:

The Notary Public may NOT give advice on legal matters unless they are attorneys.

1) While the notary public does handle written and negotiable instruments which are legal documentation, they are not permitted to draw up any legal instrumentation, which includes the drafting of wills – as these refer to the laws of succession of New York, deeds, bills of sale, mortgages, other negotiable instruments, contracts and lease agreements as these fall within the civil laws on Sales, Property, Obligations and Contracts, as well as Credit Transactions; incorporation Documents, Releases, Mechanics Liens, draft the Power of Attorney, institute complaints and other forms of litigious proceedings. Nor is the notary public authorized to draft papers for summary proceedings for the eviction of a tenant, nor intervene in bankruptcy proceedings, affidavits or any form of legal documentation that are specifically outlined as such by the judiciary.

2) This rule is not absolute however as there are specific provisions where a law student who has completed a certain amount of semesters, and law graduates who have yet to take their bar

exam may perform legal acts but only upon the supervision of a qualified lawyer in accordance with their bar association.

The Notary Public may NOT ask for and solicit legal business.
The Notary Public is expressly prohibited from the solicitation of legal business on behalf of a lawyer, or to direct constituents to a lawyer with whom they have a business relationship, or from whom they receive a form of financial remuneration or other forms of recompense for the business sent their way.

The Notary Public is NOT permitted to divide or agree to divide their fee with a lawyer. This provision also states that notaries public are not allowed to receive part of their fee from the monetary recompense of an attorney on any legal business.

The Notary Public may not advertise in or circulate in any manner, or in any document or advertisement, or claim to have any powers or privileges not granted to the notary under the statutes under which the notary was appointed.

Another activity that a notary public is not permitted to conduct is the execution of an acknowledgement of the execution of a will. The acknowledgement that arises from the notary public's acts cannot be compared to the attestation clause that comes with a will. New York Public Notary Law expressly disapproves the practice of the creation of acknowledgments and affidavits without the personal appearance of the affiant in the presence of the notary public. Remote Notarization according to the New York Department of State has other provisions.

What is Remote Notarization?

Remote notarization is a type of notarization in which the document is notarized remotely using audio-visual technology and other security standards that are appropriate for the document being notarized. Remote notarization according to the provisions can be performed by the Notary Public through traditional means – the use of pen and ink signatures, or through the use of an electronic signature.

How does Remote Notarization take Place?

For remote notarization to be valid, the notary public who performs it must be situated physically within New York State, from the moment the notarial act has been performed onto the document or instrument. The notary public must identify the remote signor (now termed as the principal) of the document through the three methods provided:

- The notary public's personal knowledge of the signor.
- Through the use of communications technology that permits the signor of an official to make a remote presentation. Credential analysis and identity proofing are used in conjunction with this to provide an accepted form of identification.
- Through the oath or affirmation of a believable witness who has personal knowledge of the signor, and who the notary public personally knows, or identified through the technology and means outlined in the previous paragraph.

Communication software may be availed of by the notaries public that they may be able to perform the requisite identity proofing and credential analysis provided for in the second method for remote notarization.

Regardless of the method utilized by the notary public, there must be a concurrence of several factors for the document that was remotely notarized to be accepted as a valid notarization:

- In real-time, the notary public must be able to see and interact with the signor through the use of the appropriate audio-visual communications technology.
- The audio-visual technology utilized must have established security protocols within its programming to ensure that there is no unauthorized access.
- The notary public must make and keep an audio-visual recording of the remote notarization. There must be a back-up copy made of the recording.

If one delves into the concept of statutory construction in the interpretation of these mandates, the use of the word must entails that these factors are mandatory in their concurrence. Any remote notarization that takes place without the concurrence of these three factors would not be accepted as valid.

What must the notary public do after the remote notarization has taken place?

Once the remote signor has executed the document, the document must be transmitted to the notary public that it may be officiated. At this point, the notary public must confirm that the document is the same as the document that was signed remotely in the presence of the notary public prior to the application of the stamp and signature of the notary upon the document. The jurat at the end of the document must contain the following phrase "This remote notarial act involved the use of communication technology."

What are Credential Analysis and Identity Proofing?

In accordance with the second condition for the consummation of the remote notarization of a document, the audiovisual communications technology utilized by the notary public must be able to perform credential analysis and identity proofing.

Credential Analysis is a method in which a third-party provider verifies a government-issued ID that the remote signor is required to present to the notary public. The government issued identification is then run by the third-party service through a review of proprietary and public data sources. Identity Proofing on the other hand is different service that is performed by a third-party service wherein the alleged identity of the remote signor is confirmed. Similar to credential analysis, the identity is ascertained when the third-party service runs the identity through public and proprietary data sources. Though these are similar in the processes that are applied to verify the identity of the remote signor, Credential Analysis serves to validate the authenticity of the identification document that is presented by the remote signor to the notary public. Identity Proofing serves to validate the identity of the remote signor.

How long should the Notary Public retain the recordings of each remote notarization?

The audio-visual recording that forms part of the mandatory requirements for the notary public must be kept by the notary for ten (10) years. Aside from this, it is the responsibility of the notary public to ensure that aside from the main recording, there must be a back-up copy made of the audio-visual recording of the remote notarizations executed. These backup copies are to be secured against unauthorized use. It is possible for the notary public to secure the services of a third party to ensure that the recordings made of the remote notarizations are retained. This latter circumstance is only permitted provided that the third party that retains the recordings on behalf of the notary public are to be made available to the Secretary of State of New York upon request.

Are notary journals for remote notarization required?

Yes. The notary public must keep a notary journal of all the remote transactions that have been performed by their person. Every journal entry must be made concurrently, or at the same time that the performance of the notarial act was performed by the notary public. For remote notarizations, the journal entry must include the date and the approximate time of the remote notarization, the name of the remote signor, the audio-visual technology that was used as the basis for the remote notarization, the number and the type of documents that have been officiated by the notary public as well as the type of notarial services that were provided. Also included in the journal entry are the identification credentials that were presented to the notary public by the remote signor. The notary journal where these remote notarizations have been documented must be retained by the notary public as long as they remain a notary, and for five years after they have ceased to be a notary.

How much can a notary public charge for remote notarization?

The notary public is permitted to charge $5.00 per act or signature. If the notary public does not perform remote notarization, the fee cannot exceed $2.00 per act.

Is Remote Notarization compulsory for all Notaries Public?

No. The service is not compulsory for all notaries public. If the notary public does not have the available technology or the capability to provide remote notarization services, or simply does not wish to take part in remote notarization, they can decline to take on remote notarizations. It is within the powers of the notary to refuse the remote notarization process if they have reason to believe that the person who is the remote signor has the capacity to sign, or if the remote signor is believed by the notary public to have signed the document officiated involuntarily or under duress.

Is there a special registration for those Notaries Public who are able to perform remote notarization?

No. The notary public that has an existent commission issued by the Secretary of State of New York may act as a traditional or remote notary. No additional or special registration is required on their part. Notaries public are not required to pay any additional fees to the Department of State or the County Clerk where the notary is duly commissioned.

NOTE: By January 31, 2023 however, notaries who wish to provide remote notarization services must register their capability to perform electronic notarizations with the New York State Department of State,

Division of Licensing Services, and then pay a fee to act as an electronic notary. There are no fees that are provided for as this will be determined through a legislative act.

Will the County Clerk or other Government Offices accept Documents that have been notarized in such a manner?

Yes. The additional legislation that provides for remote notarization states that county clerks, city registrars or other recording officers where applicable can accept for recording in their offices, a tangible copy of an electronic record of an instrument or document that is otherwise eligible to be recorded under the laws of this state as long as the record has been deemed certified by a notary public or any other individual that is authorized to perform the requested notarial act. New York Executive Law § 135-c (12) (b). For the document to be accepted by the authorities, the notary public must first certify the document that has been remotely notarized. New York Executive Law § 135-c (12) (a) provides that specific questions that pertain to the filing of such documents should be directed towards the filing office where the document will be submitted.

Under the interpretation of statutory construction, the use of the word should denote that other questions that the notary public may have with regards to the filing of the document must be directed towards the concerned office where the remotely notarized document is submitted.

12 COMPREHENSIVE GLOSSARY

Acknowledgment: A formal declaration by a signer before a notary public, affirming the authenticity of their signature.

Affidavit: A sworn statement of fact written voluntarily, witnessed, and notarized by a notary public.

Apostille: A certification from the New York Department of State that authenticates a notarized document for international use under the Hague Convention.

Certificate of Official Character: A document issued by a county clerk verifying a notary's commission for documents used outside their immediate jurisdiction.

Chattel: Personal property, such as household goods or fixtures, as defined in legal documents.

Conveyance: A legal document transferring interest in real property, such as deeds or mortgages.

Depositions: Sworn testimony taken before a trial, certified by a notary public.

Executor: A person named in a will to carry out the provisions outlined by the testator.

Impartiality: A principle requiring notaries to remain unbiased in their duties, avoiding conflicts of interest.

Jurisdiction: The geographical area where a notary public is authorized to perform notarial acts; in New York, it is statewide.

Knowledge-Based Authentication (KBA): A method of verifying a signer's identity through personal knowledge questions during remote notarizations.

Loose Certificate: A separate notarial certificate attached to a document when there is insufficient space for the notary's seal and acknowledgment.

Notarial Seal or Stamp: The official mark used to validate a notarial act, including the notary's name, commission number, and jurisdiction.

Oath: A formal promise made by an individual before a notary, affirming the truthfulness of a statement.

Perjury: A criminal offense where a person gives false testimony under oath, punishable under New York Penal Law.

Protest: A formal declaration by a notary public regarding the non-payment of a financial instrument such as a promissory note.

Remote Online Notarization (RON): A process where notarial acts are performed online using audiovisual technology to verify identities and witness signatures.

Residency Requirements: In New York, a notary must be a resident or have a place of business in the state to qualify for a commission.

Venue: The physical location of a notarial act, required to be noted in every notarial certificate.

Statutory Fee: The maximum fee a notary public can legally charge for their services, defined under New York law.

Witness: A person present at the signing of a document who can verify its execution.

13 PRACTICE TEST I

For this chapter, we are about to commence with a forty item questionnaire to determine how much more you would need to review. Earlier, we have discussed the basics of what a notary public entails, and though it would be more fruitful to do a chapter by chapter review of the entirety of notary public law, at this point, you would have read through the provisions of the notary public law provided for by New York State.

The practice exam consists of multiple choice questions. You will want to jot down your answers on a separate sheet of paper, that you may be able to check the results of your practice test afterwards. The rationale of the answers will be provided for after this examination.

To pass this practice examination, you would need to obtain a score of 28 out of 40 items to attain the passing percentage of 70 percent.

[EXAM STARTS HERE]

1) A notary public refuses to execute the notarization of an affidavit presented for New York Notary Mobile Services. What is the maximum penalty of imprisonment that may be imposed upon the notary who commits this act?
    A. 30 days
    B. 90 days
    C. Six Months
    D. One Year

2) Which of the following is in the requirements to become a Notary Public in New York State?
    A. At least has reached the age of majority
    B. Be a resident of New York or a qualified non-resident resident
    C. No special educational requirements or school level
    D. All of the above

3) Which error committed by the notary public does not invalidate the notarized document?
    A. If the Notary Public masquerades as a notary but is actually unlicensed
    B. If the commission of the Notary Public had expired when the act was performed
    C. If a New York Notary Public notarizes the document outside of their jurisdiction
    D. All of the above.

4) What is the term that refers to the location where the Notary Public has notarized a document?
    A. Venue
    B. Protest for Non-Payment
    C. Affidavit
    D. Mobile Notary

5) How much is the fee charged by the County Clerk for the Certificate of Official Character?
    A. $200
    B. No charge as the service is free to the public
    C. $5
    D. $11

6) With the exception of a will, this term refers to written instruments that transfer interests in real estate.
   A. Escrow
   B. Conveyance
   C. Duress
   D. Vendor Receipt

7) What constitutes conflict of interest in a New York Notary Public?
   A. Personal Knowledge of the Affiant
   B. When you have personal emotions towards a person
   C. When the document notarized originates from your company
   D. Legal Considerations

8) How much can a notary public charge for the issuance of protest of non-payment?
   A. $0.75 for the initial protest, with a 10 cent charge up to a limit of 5 protests
   B. $25 for an unlimited amount for a day.
   C. $5 for the original protest, with a .50 cent price for each succeeding copy
   D. $10 with a limit of $7

9) Who is the authority that is involved with the appointment of an applicant for Notary Public?
   A. The name appointed under
   B. The County Clerk
   C. Secretary of State
   D. The Judge where the Notary is domiciled.

10) In instances where there is an abandoned safety deposit box subjected to a terminated lease opening, who must accompany the bank employee to witness the act?
   A. A local law enforcer or a sheriff
   B. A bank officer or an employee of the bank
   C. The lessee who rented the safety deposit box
   D. A notary public

11) What are the repercussions for a notary who perpetrates an illegal act or commits malfeasance?
   A. Summons to a New York State Tribunal for the revocation of the notary license
   B. A hearing at a Criminal Court where the notary is the defendant
   C. Sued for monetary recompense at Civil Court

D. All of the above

12) What is referred to by Chattel?

A. Certification for Livestock as Property
B. Personal property to include household items and fixtures
C. Another term for the Jurat
D. The damages awarded for a wrongfully applied Notary Public Fee charged by a Notary Public.

13) What is an Executor?

A. A document that attests to the veracity of the authority of the Notary Public
B. The placement of a document into the hands of another person as a depositary
C. A person who is charged in a will tasked to carry out the provisions of the said will
D. An instrument that causes the modifications of the provisions of an existent will

14) For Class D Felonies, what is the maximum imprisonment penalty that may be imposed?

A. 7 years
B. 1 year
C. 3 years
D. There is no maximum jail sentence that may be imposed.

15) For Class E Felonies, what is the maximum imprisonment penalty that may be imposed?

A. 4 years
B. 7 years
C. 3 years
D. There are no limitations as this is subject to judicial discretion.

16) What is the sentence for Class 2X Felonies?

A. There is no such classification of felony
B. For a 2nd Offenses of a Class D Felony from 3 to 7 years
C. For a 1st Offenses of a Class E Felony from 3 to 4 years
D. The sentence is subject to a decision with the District Attorney and a Judge in private

17) Where can one find the Notary Public Law?
   A. The Public Officer's Law
   B. The Local Library
   C. Hearing offices of the County Clerk
   D. Authentication Offices of the County Clerk

18) Which of the following scenarios is classified as an act of Professional Misconduct?
   A. When the Notary Public consciously and knowingly performs an incorrect procedure
   B. When the Notary Public notarizes the document despite the falsity of the ID provided
   C. When the Notary Public commits a mistake and performs erroneous acts
   D. A and B

19) When a Notary is an officer of a corporation, may they notarize the documents of their own corporation?
   A. No
   B. Yes but only for employees and other corporate officers.
   C. Yes, but only if the notary is not party to the instrument individually or as a co-representative
   D. B and C

20) What is needed for an indictment for perjury that is based on an affidavit?
   A. The affiant says "I do" or words of a similar nature once the oath is read.
   B. The affiant nods their assent.
   C. The affiant affixes their thumbprint on the designated box
   D. All of the above

21) Which conditions prevent the appointment of an applicant as a Notary Public?
   A. The Notary Public has committed assault and battery
   B. The Notary Public has been convicted of possession of illegal weapons
   C. The Notary Public has committed Unlawful Entry
   D. B and C

22) May a person who is an attorney with an office in New York State, but resides outside of New York become appointed as a Notary Public within New York State?
- A. Yes. The attorney is considered as a resident of the county where their office is.
- B. Yes. The attorney, because of their profession, can automatically be appointed as a Notary.
- C. Yes. The attorney may be granted special dispensation by the Secretary of State.
- D. No. The attorney must reside in New York State to be commissioned as a Notary.

23) Which information is not included as part of the Notary Public's Identification issued by the Secretary of State?
- A. Social Security Number
- B. ID Number
- C. Commission Term
- D. Expiry Date

24) Which condition applies to members of the legislature who are notaries in the government of New York State?
- A. They are expressly forbidden from being appointed as notaries for the State.
- B. They may be notaries provided they receive no remuneration.
- C. They may be notaries as this is secondary to their function as legislators.
- D. They must resign their commission once they become legislators for the State.

25) Which of the following is an act that a notary public is allowed to perform?
- A. Execute wills of the decedent
- B. Provide legal advice on immigration
- C. Administer oaths and affirmations
- D. Represent the interests of a signor in court

26) Who among the individuals listed may not be appointed as a Notary Public in New York State?
- A. An applicant who was charged with vagrancy and granted an executive pardon
- B. A Sheriff
- C. A lawyer from New Hampshire who maintains an office in New York State

D. An applicant who was charged with prostitution and was granted a certificate of good conduct

27) When can a Notary Public re-apply for their commission without the need to undergo the Notary Public Examination?
  A. 6 months until the expiry date of their commission
  B. A year after an honorable military discharge
  C. A renewal is sent by mail to the Notary 3 months before the date of expiry of their commission
  D. All of the above

28) What are the requirements for the administration of a simple oath by the Notary Public?
  A. The person must be present in front of the Notary Public
  B. The act must be unequivocal and present
  C. Both A and B must be present
  D. Neither A and B are the answer

29) What would happen to a document if it has been notarized by a person who is not an actual Notary Public?
  A. The document would be invalidated as it is a falsified document.
  B. The document would retain its validity, but the NP will be prosecuted.
  C. The document would retain its validity, but the fake NP will be fined.
  D. None of the above

30) When is it deemed permissible to take affidavits over the phone for notarization without seeing the actual person who requested for the act?
  A. In cases of remote notarization provided the affiant appears within 24 hours.
  B. There is no circumstance that permits this because it is illegal.
  C. When the Secretary of State has given their permission to waive this requirement.
  D. When the Notary Public visits the affiant to bring the notarized document for confirmation.

31) When a Notary Public does not follow the procedures outlined, which acts are considered by the authorities that commissioned the Notary Public?
   A. The act is a serious offense
   B. The act is illegal
   C. The act will result in the removal of their license
   D. All of the above

32) Who may become a Notary Public without the need to take the Notary Public Exam?
   A. An non-resident attorney who maintains offices in Albany
   B. A Sheriff
   C. A county clerk who is part of the Unified Court System
   D. A and C

33) If a Notary Public faces suspension or removal for their misconduct, what procedure takes place first?
   A. The Notary Public is placed under house arrest while the case is resolved.
   B. The Notary Public is given a copy of the charges and allowed to be heard.
   C. The Notary Public is placed under preventive suspension.
   D. The Notary Public is permitted to file countercharges against the allegations

34) Which instances disqualify the Notary Public from the notarization of certain instruments while allowing them to remain in office?
   A. If the Notary Public stands to benefit from the action.
   B. If the Notary Public stands to gain pecuniary benefit in the action that is performed.
   C. If the Notary Public is a direct or indirect party to the transaction
   D. All of the above

35) Can the notary public be denied reappointment even if they are in good standing?
   A. No. The notary is entitled to be automatically reappointed.
   B. Yes. This is dependent upon the discretion of the Secretary of State.
   C. No. The notary is in good standing and may not be denied reappointment.
   D. Yes. The appointment is dependent upon the Secretary of Justice.

36) Which of the following is the most common notarial act performed by the Notary Public?
    A. The Execution of a Will
    B. The Issuance of Protest of Non-Payments
    C. Acknowledgments
    D. The Affirmation of Oaths

37) Which act is considered as a Class E Felony?
    A. The Issuance of a False Certificate by a Notary Public
    B. Forgery
    C. Both of them
    D. Neither of them

38) Once a document becomes notarized, what does it become in the eyes of the courts?
    A. Prima Facie Evidence
    B. Presumptive Evidence
    C. Both A and B
    D. Neither A and B

39) What is the jurisdiction of the New York State Notary?
    A. Within the county
    B. Within the country
    C. Within New York State only
    D. All of the above

40) Which of the following are not reasons why notaries are needed?
    A. Minimize fraud
    B. Prove the authenticity of signatures
    C. Compel Truthfulness
    D. Provide ready legal services to those who need it

[EXAM ENDS HERE]

14 TEST I - SOLUTIONS

This sections contains the answers and the rationales behind the answers that you may understand why the other choices are incorrect. This way, your learning experience will be enhanced as you check your answers from the first practice exam.

1) **D.** The maximum penalty prescribed is one year. Section 195.00 of the Penal Law provides that Notaries Public are bound to officiate upon request. Refusal to do so would result in the imposition of the aforementioned penalty of imprisonment for one year as the refusal to officiate upon request constitutes a misdemeanor under the said section.

2) **D.** All of the listed requirements are provided for under the New York Notary Public Law requirements. Section 130 of the provisions of Executive Law under the Notary Public Law outlines the requirements needed for applicants who wish to become notaries public in the State of New York.

3) **D.** All of the above. Commission of any of the listed offenses would result in the removal of the notarized document from the official records.

4) **A.** The term "venue" specifies the location where the notarial act occurred, as mandated by Section 137 of the Executive Law. Venue is a critical element that must be included in the certificate of acknowledgment or jurat, as it establishes the geographical jurisdiction of the notarization. Venue refers to the precise location, including the state and county, where the notarial act was performed. The notary public is authorized to perform acts statewide in New York but must include the venue specific to the county where the act was carried out. Failure to include the venue may result in the document being invalidated or contested. The venue typically appears at the beginning of the acknowledgment or jurat, using the following format: "State of New York, County of [Name of County] ss.:" This format must precede the notary's statement to clarify the location of the notarization. Under Section 137 of the Executive Law, notaries are required to include the venue in every affidavit or certificate of acknowledgment they execute. This provision ensures transparency and compliance with jurisdictional requirements. For example, if a notary performs a notarization in Manhattan (New York County), the venue would be written as follows: "State of New York, County of New York ss.:"

Notaries must never omit the venue when drafting a jurat or acknowledgment. Additionally, they should confirm the venue details before completing the notarial act to avoid errors or challenges to the document's validity.

5) **C.** The fee for a Certificate of Official Character issued by the County Clerk is $5. This fee is specified under the provisions of the Executive Law, Section 136, to ensure uniformity across New York State. For example, if a notary requests multiple certificates for different counties, each certificate incurs a separate fee of $5.

6) **B.** Conveyance. Section 290 of the Real Property Law under the Notary Public Law defines a conveyance as every written instrument or document through which any estate or any stake in real property is created, shifted, offered as security, or assigned. Conveyances are also the means by which titles to real property may be affected, which can include instruments in execution of power, though it may be of revocation only. The conveyance may also take the form of an instrument that postpones or subordinates a mortgage lien. Wills are not considered part of conveyance as the subject of wills fall under laws of succession rather than the laws of real property and carry their own separate provisions as to the disposition of the properties of the estate of the testator that made the will.

7) **D.** A conflict of interest arises when the notary has a personal or financial stake in the transaction being notarized. For instance, notarizing a document from a company where the notary is employed or stands to benefit financially would constitute a conflict of interest. This is strictly prohibited to maintain impartiality and public trust in the notary's role. Under New York Notary Public Law, notaries must avoid such situations to ensure the integrity of their actions.

8) **A.** The initial protest fee for a notary public in New York is $0.75, with an additional $0.10 charge for each subsequent protest related to the same transaction. For example, if a notary handles three protests of non-payment in one session, the total fee would be calculated as follows: $0.75 for the first protest and $0.10 each for the two additional protests, resulting in a total fee of $0.95. These fees are strictly regulated under New York law to ensure fairness and transparency in notarial services.

9) **C.** The Secretary of State. Section 130 of the Executive Law provides that the Secretary of State of New York State has the power to appoint and commission as many notaries public for New

York State in accordance with their discretion as to the notarial needs of the state, with the provision that their jurisdiction as notaries public are limited to the boundaries of the state itself.

10) **D.** The Notary Public. Section 335 of the Banking Law details the processes that an abandoned safety deposit box will undergo. If the rental fee of any safety deposit box remains unpaid, or once the lease for the said box is terminated, after 30 days of giving proper notice to the lessee (the one who leased the safety deposit box), the lessor (the bank) may, **in the presence of a notary public**, open the abandoned box and remove and take an inventory of the contents of the box. It is the responsibility of the notary public to file with the lessor a certificate under seal which attests to the date that the safety deposit box was opened, the name of the lessee and the itemized inventory of the contents. 10 days after the safety deposit box has been opened, a copy of this certificate must be mailed to the lessee at their last known postal address.

11) **D.** All of the Above. Once the notary public has committed any of the offenses listed under Section 330 of the Real Property Law, the prescribed processes that have been mentioned under these choices will then be applied. It must be reinforced that the commission of any of the offenses listed under this section would result in the liability of the notary public against the offended party.

12) **B.** According to the Definitions and General Terms outlined under Part 182: Notaries Public, Chattel is defined simply as personal property, such as household goods and fixtures.

13) **C.** An Executor, under the Definitions and General Terms outline under Part 182: Notaries Public, is defined as a person who is appointed by the testator in their will to carry out the provisions that have been subscribed by the testator onto their will.

14) **A.** Under Section 70 of the Penal Law which prescribed the maximum sentence for felonies, Class D felonies have a maximum sentence of 7 years, where the terms of the sentence are fixed by the court. Forgery is classified as a Class D Felony under these provisions under the Notary Public Law.

15) **A.** Section 70 of the Penal Laws prescribes the maximum sentence for Class E Felonies at 4 years. The terms of the sentence are to be fixed by the court. Under the provisions of the Notary Public Law, the issuance of a false certificate by the notary public is considered as a Class E Felony.

16) **A.** There is no such classification as a Class 2X Felony. Under the Section 70 and Section 70.15 of the Penal Laws in the Notary

Public Law for New York State, there are only two classifications of felonies for Notaries Public which are the Class D and Class E Felonies, and only the Class A misdemeanor.

17) **A.** The Public Officer's Law is also referred to as the Notary Public Law, and contained within its provisions are the duties and responsibilities of the notary public as a public official, as well as the provisions that are relevant to the responsibilities of their office with the relevant laws for their office.

18) **D.** All of the aforementioned choices are listed in the Notary Public Law as causes for professional misconduct. There are certain responsibilities that the notary public is expected to uphold, and there are specific actions that would penalize the notary public should they commit such acts. Due to the nature of their public office and their role in the authentication of the documents given to them to officiate, any act where the notary public engages in falsity warrants actions tantamount to professional misconduct.

19) **D.** The conditions enumerated in choices B and C are the correct answers as these are outlined in Section 138 of the Executive Law under the Notary Public Law for New York State. Notaries who are officers, or who occupy positions within corporations may notarize documents for their corporations but only under the provisions outlined in the aforementioned section.

20) **A.** Perjury under the provisions of the penal law outlined in the Notary Public Law is defined as the offense wherein a person has testified under oath or affirmation to the truth of a certain material when they actually knew that the testimony that they had made is actually false in character. In the choices that were provided, only letter A contains the part where the person who provides the testimony gives their assent to be placed under oath or affirmation, hence a false testimony from that point onwards falls under the penal definition of perjury.

21) **D.** B and C are among several offenses which can prevent the appointment of an applicant as a Notary Public in New York State. Other offenses which result in the prevention of the appointment include the possession of burglary equipment, the purchase, receipt and possession of stolen property, unlawful entry, aiding in the escape of a prisoner, the possession and distribution of narcotics, and the violation of the Selective Draft Act. Vagrancy and prostitution can also prevent the appointments but can be cured through an executive pardon or the provision of a certificate of good conduct.

22) **A** is the only answer that carries the correct conditions wherein a non-resident attorney may be appointed by the Secretary of State to be a notary public, as long as their place of business is located within a county of New York State. The other conditions do not exist, as there are no special dispensations, and immediate qualifications regardless of the residency.

23) **A.** Social Security Numbers are not included in the identification of a Notary Public. The other three choices are part of the documentation, as well as the name, address and county of the applicant.

24) **B.** Legislators are permitted to be notaries public, however, there are conditions that must be fulfilled by them. They must not receive any form of monetary compensation while commissioned as a notary public. A legislator may not hold a civil state office if they are in the position to receive monetary compensation. If they do receive remunerations, they are to vacate their seat.

25) **C.** Of the acts mentioned, notaries public are permitted to administer oaths and affirmations to those who request this service of them, and in the course of their duties. Notaries public are not permitted to execute the wills, nor are they permitted to perform any legal function related to immigration, or represent their clients in legal matters. There are disclaimers that inform clients that notaries public, except if they are attorneys, may not dispense legal advice to their clients.

26) **B.** Sheriffs are not permitted to hold any other public office due to the provisions of New York State Law. Applicants who have been charged with vagrancy and prostitution may be considered provided that they have been granted an executive pardon or a certificate of good conduct. A non-resident lawyer with offices in New York State is permitted to be a notary public.

27) **D.** All of the above are listed as conditions where a Notary Public may reapply for the renewal of their commission without the need to undertake the Notary Public Exam. These conditions are stated in Section 130 of the Executive Law of the Notary Public Law, as those applicants who fall within these conditions may have the examination requirement waived by the Secretary of State.

28) **C.** In the administration of the simplest form of oath or affirmation, it is integral that the person to whom the oath is administered to must be in the presence of the Notary Public. It is essential that the act must be unequivocal and present where the affiant takes on the obligations set forth in the oath.

29) **B.** According to Section 142-A of the Executive Laws of the Public Notary Act, documents that have been officiated by a person who purports to be a Notary Public will retain their validity regardless of the defect of the person who had authorized its notarization. However, a person is prohibited from bringing suit to this action six months after the date of notarization has passed if they had known of the defect in the validity of the notarized instrument.

30) **B.** The circumstances that govern the proper usage of remote notarization are inapplicable here as even in that instance, it is important and an essential requirement for the validity of the notarized document that the person who is the affiant or signor must make their personal appearance. Amendments to include remote notarization also add that presence must be obtained through the use of audio-visual technology, and through the use of identity proofing, and credential analysis. Presence is a component that cannot be dispensed with, and any action of notarization that does not include the presence of the affiant makes the act illegal on its onset.

31) **D.** All of the above are done by the authorities for Notaries Public who err in the procedural steps by which one should notarize a document. The Notary Public who does not follow the proper procedure will be subject to prosecution, and the revocation of their commission and license to be a Notary Public.

32) **D.** Both A and C are correct. It is stated under the New York Notary Public Law that Attorneys are not required to undertake the examination to be a Notary Public. This applies to non-resident attorneys who have offices within New York. County Clerks are also permitted to be Notaries Public as part of the Unified Court Systems. New York State Law provides that sheriffs cannot hold any other public office and are disqualified to be notaries public.

33) **B.** In accordance with the Constitutional Right for a person to due process, B is the only viable option as it allows the Notary Public to know what are the allegations made against them, and permits them to file a response that their side may be heard before the charges made against the Notary Public are resolved by the courts.

34) **D.** All of the above. Any action where the Notary Public has a vested interest, such as their ability to benefit from the effects of a transaction precludes them from the notarization of written instruments that would accrue to their benefit. This however, does not mean that the notary is disqualified from their office, rather, it means that the notary is limited in that they cannot officiate

documents wherein they are party to, and therefore benefit from the notarization of the said document.

35) **B.** It must be recalled that the commission of Notaries Public are dependent upon the discretion of the Secretary of State, not the Secretary of Justice. Regardless of the reputation and standing of the Notary Public, all commissions and appointments for Notaries Public fall within the purview of the Secretary of Justice.

36) **C.** The most common notarial act is taking acknowledgments. This act involves verifying the identity of the signer and ensuring that they signed the document willingly. Acknowledgments are frequently used in real estate transactions, such as deeds and mortgages, making them the most prevalent notarial act. Other acts, like oaths or protests, are less commonly performed.

37) **A.** Under the Penal Law provisions of the Notary Public Law, the issuance of a falsified certificate by a Notary Public is classified as a Class E Felony. This offense specifically pertains to the notary knowingly certifying a document that contains false information or was not properly executed. The classification highlights the serious nature of a notary's role in ensuring the authenticity of documents. In contrast, forgery is classified as a Class D Felony under the same penal laws. While forgery involves the creation, alteration, or use of a false document with intent to deceive, it has broader implications and is not limited to notarial acts. The distinction between these two offenses underscores the notary's responsibility to act with integrity and adhere strictly to their duties as defined by law.

38) **C.** A Notary Public employed by a corporation has the authority to perform acts related to the corporation's business, including acknowledging written instruments, protesting negotiable instruments for non-acceptance or non-payment, and taking affidavits. For example, a notary in a bank might notarize loan documents or protest a dishonored check. These powers, however, must be exercised impartially and within the scope of New York Notary Public Law.13

39) **C.** Notaries in New York are commissioned statewide, allowing them to perform notarial acts anywhere within the state. However, notaries must always include venue details that specify the state and county where the notarial act occurred. For instance, if a notarial act is performed in Queens, the venue must reflect: **"State of New York, County of Queens ss.:"** This ensures compliance with procedural standards and helps prevent jurisdictional conflicts. It is

important to note that while notaries can notarize documents outside their home county, they are not authorized to perform notarial acts outside New York State unless they hold a commission in another jurisdiction.

40) **D.** The other choices are reasons as to why notaries public are needed and commissioned by the Secretary of State of New York. Subsequently, under the provisions of the Notary Public Law of New York State, Notaries Public may not dispense legal advice as this is tantamount to professional misconduct, and their functions are limited to the notarization of documents. They are not permitted to draw up written instruments or perform other services that one would associate with an attorney.

15 PRACTICE TEST II

For this chapter, we are about to commence with a forty item questionnaire to determine how much more you would need to review. The practice exam consists of multiple choice questions. You will want to jot down your answers on a separate sheet of paper, that you may be able to check the results of your practice test afterwards. The rationale of the answers will be provided for after this examination. To pass this practice examination, you would need to obtain a score of 28 out of 40 items to attain the passing percentage of 70 percent.

[EXAM STARTS HERE]

1) The notary certificate of a witness to the execution of a real estate conveyance is referred to by what term?
   A. Qualified Resident
   B. Official Character
   C. Proof Certificate
   D. None of the Above

2) What happens if a Notary Public moves out of New York State but continues to maintain their place of work within the boundaries of the State?
   A. An additional $15 will be charged for an out of state fee
   B. The notary loses their qualifications to hold their office
   C. The notary must obtain a New York State issued Driver's License
   D. The notary is a qualified non-resident resident

3) What will you do if your neighbor asks you to notarize an affidavit?
   A. Administer an Oath of Office
   B. Administer an Oath and Complete the Jurat
   C. Require a Government-Issued, Photo Identification Document
   D. Execute a Protest for Non-Payment Certificate

4) Which of the following activities is permissible for a non-Attorney notary to perform?
   A. Explain to people the document they are signing
   B. Create a certified original certificate on a government document photocopy
   C. Draft contracts of marriage within the borders of New York State
   D. Administer an oath of office for a Military Official

5) When it is a Sunday, which of the following acts are performed by a Notary Public?
   A. Certified Original Certificate of a Government Document Photocopy
   B. Draft an Affidavit
   C. Attest to the Signatory of an Affiant for a Will by a Non-Attorney Notary
   D. Draft a Contract of Marriage

6) What is the Latin term for the words "Sworn to before me this [_] day of [_]"?
    A. Pro Se
    B. Oath
    C. Affirmation
    D. Jurat

7) What is a Deponent?
    A. One who is named in a will who carries out its provisions
    B. The testimony of a witness taken out of court while under oath or affirmation
    C. An agreement
    D. A person who is ordered to a hearing in a deposition

8) What is the item that a Notary Public places below their Signature?
    A. Seal
    B. Stamp
    C. Statement of Authority
    D. Certification

9) How much is the fee for the change of name due to marriage to update the State?
    A. $10 for a Change from the Previous Legal Name
    B. Free for anyone who changes their name due to marriage
    C. $5 for the update of the database
    D. $12 single charge fee

10) Who may translate a deed into another language, that it may be filed in a New York County Clerk's office?
    A. A Translator with a certificate of designation by the county judge
    B. A Translator with the credentials from a reputable translation company
    C. An Affidavit Service Magistrate
    D. All of the Above

11) What is signed by the two witnesses to a will?
    A. The witness approval certificate of proof
    B. Attestation Clauses
    C. Identity Verification Form
    D. Affidavit

12) Who is the authority responsible for the issuance of certificates for various Notaries Public Procedures?
- A. Office of the County Clerk
- B. Office of the Secretary of State
- C. Office of the Notary Public
- D. All of the Above

13) How much is the fee charged for an affidavit at the County Clerk's office?
- A. $2.00
- B. $2.00 for every original signature witnessed
- C. .75 cents for the first affidavit and .10 cents for the succeeding affidavit
- D. There is no charge as notarial services are free during office hours

14) What is the maximum sentence for Class A Misdemeanors?
- A. 1 year
- B. 5 years
- C. 3 years' probation
- D. 6 months imprisonment

15) What is the mandatory sentence for a Class D Felony Conviction?
- A. 4 years
- B. 7 years
- C. 3 years
- D. This is a matter of judicial discretion and there is no mandatory sentence.

16) What is an Apostille?
- A. An instrument certified for international use
- B. A term for notary application
- C. A Class D Felony
- D. The Court-Appointed Administrator of a Will

17) When the County Clerk issues an Authentication Certificate and charges a $3 fee, what was completed?
- A. Verified that the affiant is a registered voter
- B. Verified that the signature of the Notary Public is authentic
- C. Certified the involvement of the Notary Courts
- D. All of the above

18) Which of the following individuals may hold the office of a Notary Public?
  - A. A County Sheriff
  - B. A former Commissioner of Deeds for New York City who was removed from their office
  - C. A and B
  - D. A Convicted Felon

19) Who are those individuals permitted to have a limited practice of law as a non-attorney?
  - A. Law students who have taken 2 semesters and have not failed their bar exams twice.
  - B. Prevention of Cruelty officers
  - C. You when you represent yourself
  - D. All of the above

20) What is referred to by Laches?
  - A. A device that secures the Notary Journal away from the Public
  - B. An instance where one attains too many traffic violations
  - C. A term that refers to the delay or negligence in the assertion of one's rights in court
  - D. None of the above

21) Which of these offenses would warrant the prevention of the appointment of an applicant to a Notary Public Commission?
  - A. Illegal Possession of Firearms
  - B. Non-Payment of Debt
  - C. Harassment
  - D. Prostitution

22) Which of these events takes place when a Notary Public moves out of their New York Residence and does not retain any office or business in the state?
  - A. They retain their commission but cannot notarize documents.
  - B. Their commission is rendered vacant as they no longer qualify to hold their office
  - C. They retain their commission as non-resident notaries
  - D. They have to pay a fee to be allowed to notarize documents while out of state

23) What happens when a Notary Public's Identification has been destroyed or damaged?
- A. They may request a replacement card for free from the County Clerk
- B. The County Clerk will charge a fee of $10 to make a duplicate identification card
- C. The Secretary of State will charge a fee of $10 to issue a card with duplicate on it
- D. None of the above

24) How much is the fee charged when the Notary Public has changed their name or address on file?
- A. $10
- B. It is free for all notaries public
- C. $3
- D. $5

25) What happens if a former Commissioner of Deeds, who has been removed from office, notarizes documents, despite knowledge that they have been removed from their position?
- A. The documents will retain their notarial validity
- B. The former Commissioner will be reprimanded.
- C. The former Commissioner will be guilty of a misdemeanor
- D. Both A and C

26) What will happen if a Commissioner of Elections or Inspector of Elections becomes a Notary Public?
- A. They will be removed from office as they are forbidden to hold public office.
- B. Their position as a Commissioner of Elections will be vacated in favor of their new office.
- C. Their commission as a Notary Public is perfectly valid and they may execute its functions
- D. They will be banned from any other public office

27) Which of these practices are applicable to advertising practices for Notaries Public in New York State?
- A. Attorneys at law are subject to the advertising limitations in the Notary Public Law
- B. Notaries Public are required to issue a translated disclaimer that shows that they are not attorneys, nor are they allowed to provide legal advice on any other matters.

C. Notaries Public may use terms in other languages to indicate that they may provide legal advice.

D. Infractions of these regulations will result in a fine of $500.

28) An acknowledgement of proof of a conveyance of real estate may be made in the presence of all but one of the following officials?

A. A notary public

B. An official examiner of title

C. A justice of the Supreme Court

D. A former Commissioner of Deeds removed from office

29) When is a notary public authorized to solemnize a marriage or execute a contract of marriage?

A. When the Notary Public has personal knowledge of the bride and groom

B. When the Notary Public has been given a permit by the Secretary of State

C. The Notary Public is not authorized in any circumstance to perform such an act

D. The Notary Public has to apply for a special authorization to perform an act.

30) Who may institute a proceeding against a Notary Public who engaged in the illegal practice of law?

A. By Motion of the Supreme Court

B. By Motion of the Officers charged with the investigation of the illegal practice of law

C. By Motion of any Bar Association incorporated within New York State

D. All of the Above

31) When a notary public makes an acknowledgment of proof of a conveyance of real estate, it cannot be made in the presence of which of these officials?

A. Justice of the Peace

B. Town Councilman

C. A Justice of an Inferior Court

D. Town Sheriff

32) Which of these acts constitutes the commission of Forgery in the 2nd Degree?
    A. If a Notary Public executes a written instrument that affects the legal right of another
    B. If a Notary Public does not execute a document that is to be of public record
    C. If a Notary Public does not execute a document that is issued by a public office
    D. None of the above

33) Which of these are considered as a requisite of acknowledgements?
    A. The person who executes the instrument signs in the presence of the notary
    B. The proof or knowledge of the notary that the person who makes the acknowledgment is the one in their presence
    C. The person who makes the acknowledgment has two witnesses to attest to its execution
    D. All of the above

34) When is a notary disqualified to take the acknowledgment of a grantor or mortgagor?
    A. When the Notary has personal knowledge of the grantor or mortgagor
    B. When the Notary is a grantee of the grantor or mortgagor
    C. When the Notary themselves are the grantor
    D. Both B and C

35) When a notary does make the acknowledgment of a conveyance wherein, they have a personal financial interest, what happens to the acknowledgment?
    A. The acknowledgment executed becomes nullified on its face as it was illegal on its onset
    B. The acknowledgment will stand as this would prejudice the rights of the other parties
    C. The acknowledgment executed becomes the subject of a separate civil action
    D. The acknowledgment will stand as this is generally permitted by Notary Public Law

36) When is fraud in office committed?
  A. When a person publicly acts as a notary public without any commission
  B. When a notary public executes an act with the intent to deceive
  C. When a commissioner of deeds performs an act with the intent to defraud
  D. All of the above

37) Which of these advertising methods are deemed permissible by New York Notary Public Law?
  A. Television Advertisements
  B. Business Cards
  C. Billboards
  D. Word of Mouth from other Attorneys

38) What are the powers of the Notary Public who is an employee of a corporation?
  A. They may protest for non-acceptance or non-payment
  B. They may protest for the collection of negotiable instruments held by a corporation
  C. They may take the acknowledgment of a written instrument of such corporation
  D. All of the above

39) Which of these defects would invalidate the notarized document if found to be present?
  A. The name of the notary has been misspelled in the commission
  B. The notary was ineligible to be commissioned by the Secretary of State
  C. The commission of the notary has expired at the time of the notarial act.
  D. None of the above

40) Which of these provisions apply to the acknowledgments or proofs made by married women?
  A. It may be made by the woman as though she is unmarried
  B. She is required to adhere to specific laws regarding the partition of marital property
  C. This is dependent upon the provisions of their pre-nuptial agreement
  D. None of the above

[EXAM ENDS HERE]

16   TEST II - SOLUTIONS

This sections contains the answers and the rationales behind the answers that you may understand why the other choices are incorrect. This way, your learning experience will be enhanced as you check your answers from the first practice exam.

1) **C.** The Proof Certificate under the Notary Public Law of New York State is classified as an acknowledgment of proof under Section 298 of the Real Property Laws. Furthermore, under Section 306 which contains the provisions for the acknowledgment of proof, the person who takes the acknowledgment or the instrument that proves conveyance is obligated to validate or assign a certificate signed by themselves, which states all of the provisions that are to be done, known or proven when the instrument of acknowledgment or proof was taken by the individual. This must be accompanied by the name and the substantial testimony of each witness that was examined before the person; and if the person who requested proof is a subscribing witness, they must indicate their place of residence.

2) **D.** The provisions on the residential qualifications for a Notary Public are enshrined within Section 130 of the executive law, where it is provided that a notary public who is a resident of the State, but moves out of New York though continues to retain a business or office in the State does not vacate their commission as a notary public.

3) **B.** There are no preclusions that prevent a Notary Public from the execution of an affidavit for their neighbor, thus it is important that the Notary Public comply with the procedural steps in the completion of an affidavit. Hence, it is imperative that the Notary Public comply with the Jurat once they have administered the requisite oath. All other options are inapplicable to the situation with your neighbor as it is not stated that they are to take office, nor have they requested a protest of non-payment.

4) **D.** The administration of oaths are the only function a non-Attorney notary may perform from the choices listed as all other actions entail the involvement of legal processes which are among the four prohibited actions that a notary should not perform. The notary may officiate documents however they are not permitted to explain the contents of an officiated instrument to the parties as this constitutes a legal consultation due to the nature of the instrument. Notaries who are not attorneys are not permitted to draft any form of legal

instrumentation which includes certifications of government issued documents as well as the creation of marriage contracts as these are all legal instruments, that fall within the performance of legal practice, still prohibited by the rules on conduct of the Notary Public Law for New York State.

5) **B.** Under the Rules and Regulations of Title 19, NYCRR, Chapter V, Subchapter L, Part 182 for Notaries Public, there are specialized instructions as to the functions a Notary Public may perform on a Sunday. Notaries public are permitted to administer an oath, take an affidavits or acknowledgements. What notaries public cannot do on a Sunday is to take a deposition for a civil proceeding. Hence, B is the only permissible action. In addition to this, all other choices that have been presented are prohibited under the Rules of Conduct as these constitute the performance of legal actions.

6) **D.** The Jurat is simply the section of an affidavit wherein it is certified by the notary that an affidavit was sworn and taken before their presence. This means that the jurat, in accordance with the definition provided by the Rules and Regulations of Title 19, NYCRR, Chapter V, Subchapter L, Part 182 for Notaries Public, is not the affidavit but part of the affidavit.

7) **D.** In the list of definitions provided for by the Rules and Regulations of Title 19, NYCRR, Chapter V, Subchapter L, Part 182 for Notaries Public, a Deponent is one who makes an oath to a written statement, hence, one who is ordered to participate in a deposition. The term is interchangeable with the word affiant.

8) **C.** Section 137 of the Executive Law under the Notary Public Law has the provisions for the Statements as to the Authority of the Notary Public. In addition to the venue and the signature of the notary public, the notary public must print or typewrite or stamp, beneath their signature in blank ink (the signature should be in black), and their name, the words "Notary Public State of New York", the name of the county in which the Notary Public is permitted to practice, and the expiry date of their commission as a notary public. Whenever required, the notary public is to include the name of any county in which their certificate of official character is filed, with the phrase "Certificate filed ....County". If the Notary Public is an Atty or a Counselor at Law, they may at their discretion substitute "Attorney and Counselor at Law" for the words "Notary Public". The other choices listed have not been mentioned within the outlined provisions.

9) **B.** While the provisions of the Notary Public Law have fees for the change of name, but for reasons of marriage, this fee is not exacted from the Notary Public. There are certain rules that must be followed however, but otherwise no fees are charged from them.

10) **A.** Section 333 of the Real Property Law provides that documents that require translation into the English language be attended to by a translator duly designated for such purpose by the county judge of the county where it is preferred to record such a conveyance or a Supreme Court Justice. The translated document must be duly signed, acknowledged, and certified under oath, or upon confirmation by such a person before such judge, that the translation made is true and accurate, and it should contain a certification of the designation of the said person by the judge.

11) **B.** In the creation of a will, which notaries public and prospective applicants must be reminded is a purely legal act, the provisions within the drafted will are attested to by the witnesses to the drafting of the said will. It must be reiterated at this point that notaries public cannot execute the acknowledgment of the execution of a will. This action if performed cannot be deemed equal to an attestation clause that forms the basis of the will. The attestation clause as defined by the Rules and Regulations of Title 19, NYCRR, Chapter V, Subchapter L, Part 182 for Notaries Public, is the clause located at the end of the will where the witnesses to the creation of the will of the testator certify that the instrument was executed in their presence as well as the manner by which the will has been executed.

12) **D.** There are various provisions throughout the Notary Public Law that outline the authorities who may issue certifications for various notarial services. Aside from the apparent alternative of the Office of the Notary Public, certain notarial services may be acquired via the offices of the County Clerk, with associated fees. The Office of the Secretary of State is also permitted to issue certificates at the request of a notary public, as the notary public's notarial powers originate from the Secretary of State of New York. So they are also authorized for these types of transactions.

13) **D.** Section 534 of County Law provides that each county clerk shall entitle from among the members of their staff, at least one notary public to be open for the notarization of documents in each office of the county clerk during normal business hours free of charge. Each individual appointed in such an instance pursuant to Section 534 of County Law shall be exempt from the payment of the

application and examination fees required by Section 131 of the Executive Law in the Notary Public Laws.

14) **A.** Section 70.15 of the Penal Laws listed under the Notary Public Law for New York State contain the provisions for Sentences of Imprisonment for Misdemeanors and Violations. This question asks about the maximum sentence of imprisonment for those who have committed Class A Misdemeanors. The penal laws provide that the sentence shall be definite, which means that the sentence is to have a fixed date, determined by the courts. Sentences for these types of misdemeanors shall not exceed a period of one year.

15) **C.** Section 70 of the Penal Laws listed under the Notary Public Law for New York State has the provisions for the Sentence of Imprisonment for Felonies. It must be impressed upon the applicant who takes this examination that there is a maximum term of sentence which is dependent on the type of felony. This question refers to the classifications of felonies wherein there is an indeterminate sentence, and under these provisions, the maximum sentence that may be imposed shall be at least three years.

16) **A.** An apostille is defined by the glossary of terms under the Rules and Regulations of Title 19, NYCRR, Chapter V, Subchapter L, Part 182 for Notaries Public, where it is an authentication that stems from the Department of State that is then attached to a notarized and county-certified document that makes the document usable for international purposes.

17) **B.** Section 133 of the Executive Law contains provisions relating to notarial signatures, which states that the clerk of a county in whose office a notary public has qualified or filed their handwritten signature and certificate of an official character upon request and payment of the fee of $3. Such person shall affix to any certificate of proof of acknowledgment or oath signed anywhere in the State of New York a certificate under his hand and seal. Such certificate shall state that a commission or certificate of his official character with his handwritten signature was filed in their office and that the county clerk was duly authorized to take it. Furthermore, such a certificate shows the handwriting of such a notary to permit a comparison with the signature on the certificate of proof of acknowledgment or oath with the handwritten signature deposited in their office by the notary. This control is used to verify the authenticity of the signature. This instrument, with the certification of the county clerk affixed to it, may be read as evidence or

recorded in any county in the State of New York for which a certificate of the county clerk may be required for either purpose.

18) **D.** There may be issues with this answer, contentious as it may be, so it becomes necessary to qualify the other answers first. A sheriff may never be a notary public as they are prohibited by New York State Constitutional Law, Section 13(a), Article 13. A general rule that disqualifies a notary from the actions of a notary public provides that if a notary forms part of the transaction or has a direct and monetary interest in the transaction, the notary cannot be capable of action in that case. Section 140 of the Executive Law provides that Commissioners of Deeds for the City of New York who have been removed from office are ineligible for reappointment as commissioners or notaries public. Given this, it must be reasoned out that D, as a convicted felon is the only answer. This answer however, has to be qualified in itself, as a general rule is that no person who has been convicted of a crime shall be eligible to hold office as a notary public. However, despite this, unless the Secretary makes a finding in conformance with all applicable statutory requirements, including those contained in Article 23(a) of the Corrections Law, that such convictions do NOT constitute a bar to appointment. From this it can be interpreted through the construction of the provision, that it is possible for a convicted felon to be a notary public.

19) **D.** It must be reiterated that notaries public who are not attorneys are prohibited from the practice of law. *People vs. Alfani* 227 NY 334,339 given that legal guidance and advice, the drafting of agreements, the establishment of corporations and the preparation of corporate papers, and the drafting of all types of legal documents, including wills, are activities that have been regarded to be part of the practice of law. Section 484 of Judicial Law however, under the Notary Public Law provides that all of the choices that have been mentioned here, are permitted to practice in a limited capacity. It must be reiterated however that with regards to the practice of law students who have undertaken the two semester requirements, that they be only allowed to perform their limited practice once they have taken their bar examinations immediately available upon their graduation from law school, or have failed but are within the two examination limit provided for under Section 484. They must also act under the supervision of a legal aid organization which would determine the limits to which students may render legal practice to the extent determined by their authorities. Section 1403 of the Not-

for-Profit Corporation Law allow for officers of societies for the prevention of cruelty to engage in a limited practice of law, but only within the limited extent that was outlined in the said section. It is also permissible, to engage in the limited practice of law, when the applicant, or the notary public, engages in it for their self-interest.

20) **C.** Laches is a term that can simply be interpreted as the delay or negligence in the assertion of one's rights according to the Rules and Regulations of Title 19, NYCRR, Chapter V, Subchapter L, Part 182 for Notaries Public. It is termed as an equitable defense that may be raised by the defendant in that the one who invokes its defense asserts that the claimant has delayed in the assertion of their rights, and because of the delay, is no longer entitled to bring an equitable claim. When this defense is raised, the failure to assert one's rights in a timely manner can results in claims being barred by laches, hence the estoppel by laches application. It is believed that equity aids those who are vigilant and not the negligent. This is not absolute however, in that delay does not prevent a claimant from obtaining relief. It must be made however that there is a difference between the application of laches and the application of the statute of limitations as the latter prevents the party from the assertion of claims after the period in which they could file their action has passed.

21) **A.** The possession of illegal firearms is one of the convictions that bars a person from their appointment as a Notary Public in New York State. Other offenses include illegal entry, the possession and sale of stolen goods, burglary, and assistance in the escape of prisoners, the possession of illegal drugs as well as violations of the selective draft act. While Prostitution may be considered as an offense that can preclude the appointment of a person, it can be pardoned or waived by a certificate of good conduct. The other choices do not constitute an absolute ban on the appointment of a notary public.

22) **B.** Notaries public for them to retain their commission once they are outside of the State, must maintain an office or a place of business within the State. If they are unable to do so, or are disinterested in the retention of their commission, their commission and their office as a notary is vacated as they no longer have jurisdiction or meet the venue requirement needed of them to maintain their status as a Notary Public.

23) **C.** Section 131 (13) of the Executive Law of the Notary Public Law states that a duplicate identity card may be issued by the Secretary

of State after the payment of a non-refundable $10 fee and the submission of an application form. Subsequently, the identification card that has been issued will contain the same number for the Notary Public, as well as the word Duplicate stamped across the face of the Notary Public.

24) **A.** Section 131 (12) of the Executive Law of the Notary Public Law states that the Secretary of State will charge a non-refundable fee of $10 when the notary public changes their name or their address. This fee is not charged when the changes are made in an application for reappointment.

25) **D.** Both A and C detail the circumstances of a notarial procedure that has been executed by a former Commissioner of Deeds who has been removed from office. Section 140 of Executive Law provides that once there has been knowledge of the act performed by the said person, the former Commissioner will be found guilty of a misdemeanor. They are not reprimanded in the manner that one would be scolded, as the charges of a misdemeanor involve the imposition of a prison sentence to be fixed by the courts.

26) **C.** Sections 3-200 and 3-400 of the Election Law under the Notary Public Law provide that a Commissioner of Elections or an Inspector of Elections may hold office as a notary public. The ban on other public offices applies only to the Sheriff as this is provided for in the Constitutional Law of New York State. The other choices do not constitute valid answers.

27) **B.** Attorneys are not subject to the advertising requirements provided for in Section 135-b. What the section does provide is that notaries public are required to issue a disclaimer translated into a foreign language that they are not attorneys and that they may not give legal advice in the United States. Subsequently, by virtue of the previous statement, the translations must be exact and not use terms that imply that the notary public is licensed to practice law in the United States or that they are permitted to give legal advice on immigration. Violations of this provision will result in a fine of a thousand dollars, not $500.

28) **D.** It must be recalled that former Commissioners of Deeds who have been removed from office are prohibited from the execution of any notarial act. Hence, under the provisions of Section 298 of the Real Property Law, the acknowledgment mentioned in this question may be made in the presence of A, B and C, as well as an official referee, at any place within the State.

29) **C.** Under Section 11 of the Domestic Relations Law, a Notary Public has no authority to solemnize a marriage nor are they permitted to acknowledge the parties or witnesses to a written contract of marriage. There are no exceptions or special provisions that permit the Notary Public from the performance of these acts.

30) **D.** All of the parties concerned in the three choices are permitted to initiate proceedings against Notaries Public who have engaged in the illegal practice of law, in accordance with the provisions from Section 750 under the Judiciary Laws of the Notary Public Law of New York State. The Supreme Court of New York has the jurisdiction to punish for criminal contempt any person who engages in the illegal practice of law.

31) **D.** Under Section 298 (3) of the Real Property Law of the Notary Public Law of New York State, Town Sheriffs are not among the officials listed in this provision. In the aforementioned provision it is noted that an acknowledgment or proof of conveyance of real estate may be executed in the presence of several officials, but where these officials are unavailable, it may be done in the presence of the local justice of the peace, a justice of an inferior court (to say that is, justices from the local courts, or any court lower in rank to the Supreme Court), and a town councilman. While there is no provision for a town sheriff, there is a provision that the village police chief may be a witness to the acknowledgment or proof of the conveyance of real property made.

32) **A.** Section 170.10 of the Penal Laws contains the provisions for Forgery in the 2nd Degree which is a Class D Felony. The Notary Public who is found guilty of this felony has committed the actions wherein, with the intent to deceive, defraud or injure another party, the notary falsely simulates or alters a written instrument purported to be one that affects the legal rights of another party such as a will, codicil or contract; or if they execute documents that form part of the records of public offices or are generally issued by public offices as part of the public record.

33) **B.** Section 303 of the Real Property Law is the source of the answer for this question wherein it is provided that that the most important requisite for the execution of an acknowledgment is the knowledge or proof on the part of the notary public that the person who requested for the acknowledgment is who they say they are. Proof of identity becomes an important aspect when the Notary Public needs to ascertain the identity and this can be done through credential verification and identity proofing, procedures of which

may be applied by the Notary Public when they are unsure or wish to ascertain the identity of a person. Subsequently, choice A, while present in the same section, is not considered as an essential element in the execution of acknowledgment. This means that it is not necessarily required for the requesting party to sign in the presence of the notary public, though admittedly, when one interprets this, it seems to be an unavoidable act. Regardless, this element may be dispensed with if the circumstances are indeed encountered by the Notary Public. Choice C is not among the circumstances listed as a requisite for the execution of an acknowledgment.

34) **D.** Under the Miscellaneous Provisions of the New York Notary Public Law, there is a general rule that provides for the preclusion of notaries public from the execution of an acknowledgment when they stand to benefit from its execution. This means that the notary public cannot take part in the acknowledgment of written instruments wherein they have a financial stake. In the choices listed, Both B and C are situations wherein the notary stands to gain a financial benefit as either they themselves are able to ease the requirements and fast track their paperwork to ensure that they get the remuneration that they need, or that they are able to ensure that as grantors, they would be able to benefit when another person subjects themselves to the notary public as the mortgagee. This entails that the notary public used their own office for personal gain, an act which is generally prohibited given that the office of the Notary Public is meant to serve the interests of the public, not of themselves. Hence, it is both B and C that serve as situations that would preclude the notary public.

35) **A.** The Miscellaneous Provisions of the New York Notary Public Law contain several provisions on what would disqualify the notary public from the execution of several types of written instruments when they stand to financially gain from it once the acknowledgment from these instruments has been executed by them. In the event that the notary public did attempt to circumvent the provisions, it was held by the rulings of the courts of New York that the acknowledgment that was executed by the notary public will be nullified from the start, as it was never legal to begin with. As such, this defect in the acknowledgment will be fatal and thus cannot be held to be legally binding upon the parties concerned, which makes A the only correct choice. However, there is a remedy when the acknowledgment becomes nullified due to the defect on

the part of the notary public as they would be liable for malfeasance, and thus be personally liable to the affected parties in this case. The Notary Public who stands to benefit financially from the acknowledgment causes the executed document to be nullified, and it would have no legal effect.

36) **D.** In accordance with the provisions under Section 135-a of the Penal Laws, all of these acts are considered fraud in office when committed by a person who purports themselves to be commissioner of deeds or notary public without the actual commission from the Secretary of State or when the Notary Public or Commissioner of Deeds engages in acts that carry the intent to deceive or defraud their constituents. To be specific, the acts for the former circumstance wherein the person masquerades themselves a duly commissioned notary public when they are not include the performance of the functions of these two offices, who assumes the title from another person, uses the title of notary public, or even advertises themselves to be notaries public. These are not limited to these circumstances as any act wherein a person pretends to be a notary public or a commissioner of deeds sans the actual commission constitute fraud in office. Subsequently, violations that result in fraud of office would result in a misdemeanor on the offender.

37) **B.** Business Cards, among the choices listed are among the permissible forms of advertisement for a Notary Public. Other permissible forms include the use of brochures and notices whether in print or electronic form. Television advertisements are not among the permitted media for notaries public, and neither are billboards. Advertisements according to Section 135-b (4) include materials that are meant to give notice or promote the services of a notary public. While in essence A, B and C fulfill this definition, only B is given the requisite permissibility as a form of advertisement. Subsequently, choice D is an illegal act which results in the commission of an act of professional misconduct on the part of the Notary Public as they are not permitted to engage in the active solicitation of businesses through lawyers, nor are lawyers permitted to solicit businesses through the services of a notary public.

38) **D.** Section 138 of the Executive Law provides that a Notary Public, among the various officials listed in this provision, may perform the functions that have been listed in the choices for this question. It is possible for a Notary Public who has been employed in a

corporation to take the acknowledgments of written instruments that have originated from the said corporation. They are also permitted to administer the oath of any other stockholder, director, officer or employee of the corporation that they work for. In addition to these functions, it is possible for the notary public to issue protests for the non-acceptance or non-payment- subject to the rules provided for in the Notary Public Law, to include bills of exchange, drafts, notes and other instruments that may be categorized under the legal definition of negotiable instruments – provided that these are held by a corporation.

39) **D.** None of the above. Section 142-a, provides for the validities of the acts of a notary public and commissioners of deeds despite the presence of certain defects. The defects that would not invalidate a notarial act despite their presence, include: The ineligibility of the commissioner of deeds or notary public to be appointed as such (subsequently, this means that they should not even carry the title). This is different however, from the offense where a person purports themselves to be a notary public when they are not, as in the first circumstance, there seems to be an implied application that was submitted, but was not approved. The same circumstance can also happen if a notary public who was in good standing simply was not recommissioned by the Secretary of State upon their personal discretion. In the latter circumstance where the person purports themselves to be a notary public, this was an act with the intent to deceive the public into the payment for fraudulent services and is an entirely different circumstance. Another defect that is addressed by this section includes events where the name of the notary public or the commissioner of deeds has been misspelled. The presence of the misspelled name does not constitute a fatal defect and can be easily remedied with a correction of the notary public's name. When the notary public or commissioner of deeds fails to take their oath, or file their oath, or qualify themselves for their office, this does not invalidate the document that was notarized. The notarized document retains its validity even if the term of the commission of the notary public or commissioner of deeds has expired. This implies that there is no retroactive application of the expiry. Even if the notary public has vacated their office through a change of their residence, or if the notary public has taken another public office, or has committed any other action that results in the vacation of their offices as notary public, the document will still retain its validity. Lastly, though the notarial act may have been performed

outside of the jurisdiction of the notary public or the commissioner of deeds, it would still retain its validity. The presence of these defects are not absolute in their application that all documents and written instruments that have been notarized automatically retain their validity despite their presence. It is noted within the provisions of the same section that if the signor or affiant knows of the presence of these defects and persists with their action in the notarization of the document, they may not assert the terms of what was listed in the document. This means that if the one who notarized document knew that the circumstances in which the document was flawed in the validity of the notary public, they cannot claim or institute actions that would enforce the terms of the document that they had notarized. They cannot claim that their document retains their validity if they knew that their defect was existent in such a manner. This circumstance however will not apply after six months had passed from the date of the notarial act.

Once six months have passed, the validity may be asserted but only to the extent that the defect enacted by the notary public or commissioner of deeds failed to state the date or venue where the act was done.

It must be noted by all notaries public and those who intend to apply, that despite the validity of the documents that result from such defects, this section does not absolve the notary public of criminal or civil liability. This does not also enlarge their authorities to act beyond the functions that have been provided for within the provisions of the Notary Public Law.

40) **A.** In this instance there is no need to complicate matters with the introduction of the marriage contract as well as the involvement of property laws as this would involve an illegal practice of law by the notary public who is a non-attorney. As it is, under the provisions of Section 302 of the Real Property Law under the Notary Public Laws of New York State, married women may make acknowledgments and proofs within the state, the same method as though they were unmarried.

17 CONCLUSION & BONUS

Embarking on the journey to become a New York Notary Public is both a challenging and rewarding endeavor. This guide has equipped you with the essential knowledge and tools needed to navigate the process—from understanding the foundational principles of notarization to mastering the legal and ethical responsibilities of a notary. As a notary public, you play a vital role in upholding the integrity of critical transactions. Your duties extend beyond mere administrative tasks; they embody trust, professionalism, and commitment to public service. Whether notarizing real estate agreements, administering oaths, or certifying legal documents, your expertise ensures that the principles of fairness and authenticity are upheld. This guide also serves as a launchpad for a fulfilling career or an enhancement to your existing professional journey. Your commitment to excellence in notarial services will not only foster personal growth but also contribute significantly to your community. With determination and proper preparation, success in the New York Notary Public Exam is within reach. Embrace the opportunities ahead and step confidently into your role as a trusted public servant. Remember, your efforts today lay the foundation for a career marked by professionalism and public trust. Best of luck on your notarial journey!

YOUR FEEDBACK MATTERS

If you found this guide helpful, please consider leaving an honest review on Amazon. Your feedback not only helps improve this book but also supports others on their journey to becoming a notary public.

BONUS

Scan the following QR code to be directed to a web page where you can access 19 incredible bonuses: 10 online courses to enhance and test your knowledge about New York Notary Public exam, 6 different packets of digital (online) and printable (pdf) flash cards about the topic and 3 mobile apps helpful for your profession of Notary Public.

Link: https://dl.bookfunnel.com/y9qycdvpiz